ALL CLEAR

Listening and Speaking

Helen Kalkstein Fragiadakis

HEINLE
CENGAGE Learning

Australia • Brazil • Japan • Korea • Mexico • Singapore • Spain • United Kingdom • United States

HEINLE
CENGAGE Learning™

All Clear 3
Listening and Speaking
Helen Kalkstein Fragiadakiss

Publisher, Academic ESL: James W. Brown

Executive Editor, Dictionaries and
   Adult ESL: Sherrise Roehr

Director of Content Development:
   Anita Raducanu

Associate Development Editor:
   Katie Carroll

Associate Development Editor:
   Jennifer Meldrum

Director of Product Marketing:
   Amy Mabley

Senior Field Marketing Manager:
   Donna Lee Kennedy

Associate Marketing Manager:
   Caitlin Driscoll

Senior Production Editor:
   Maryellen E. Killeen

Senior Print Buyer: Betsy Donaghey

Project Manager: Tunde Dewey

Composition: Parkwood Composition

Interior Design: Lori Stuart

Artist: Steve Haefele

ISBN-13: 978-1-4130-1705-2

ISBN-10: 1-4130-1705-3

ISE ISBN-13: 978-1-4130-2099-1

ISE ISBN-10: 1-4130-2099-2

Heinle
20 Channel Center Street
Boston, MA 02210
USA

Cengage Learning is a leading provider of customized learning solutions
with office locations around the globe, including Singapore, the United
Kingdom, Australia, Mexico, Brazil, and Japan. Locate your local office at
www.cengage.com/global

Cengage Learning products are represented in Canada by
Nelson Education, Ltd.

Visit Heinle online at **elt.heinle.com**

Visit our corporate website at **www.cengage.com**

Printed in the United States of America
14 15 16 22 21 20 19

To my family, yesterday and today—

Acknowledgements

The original *All Clear* idioms text came out more than twenty years ago, and the additional two texts at higher and lower levels appeared years later. It was always my dream for these three texts to become a comprehensive listening and speaking series using idioms and other expressions as springboards for activities, and I have many people to thank for making this dream come true.

To Jim Brown, publisher, and Sherrise Roehr, executive editor, thank you for getting the ball rolling on this project. To Katie Carroll and Jennifer Meldrum, my developmental editors, thank you for your wonderful attention and detailed suggestions. To Maryellen Eschmann-Killeen and the rest of the production team, thank you for your enthusiasm and creativity.

I would also like to express my gratitude to the many colleagues who over the years gave me extremely valuable feedback, which I incorporated into the new editions. I would especially like to thank Inocencia Dacumos, Rosemary Loughman, Helen Munch, Kathleen Pappert, Ellen Rosenfield, and Larry Statan.

A big thank you goes to my daughter Melissa, who for years has enthusiastically given me feedback to help make the language in *All Clear* dialogues as natural as possible. Thank you, Melissa, for using your wonderful sense of *what people really say* to answer such questions as "How would you say this?", "Would you ever say that?", "Does this sound natural?", and "What's another way to say. . . ?"

I would also like to thank my many students for their interest and insightful questions as I taught with the *All Clear* texts. While teaching, I jotted down your questions in the textbook margins. And then, while revising the texts, I used your questions as guides to improve the material.

Finally, I would like to thank Michael Lewis, who has put the lexical approach in the center stage of language acquisition. I wrote the first *All Clear* in the early 1980's, and ten years later it was a revelation to hear Lewis talk about the value of teaching "chunks" of language—collocations and fixed expressions. I have found that focusing on lexical items (many, but not all of them, idiomatic) in a natural dialogue can provide concrete material that can serve as a springboard for numerous activities in a listening/speaking class. Thank you, Michael Lewis, for bringing the lexical approach to the forefront of language teaching and learning.

Helen Kalkstein Fragiadakis
March, 2006

CONTENTS

CONTENTS

CONTENTS

CONTENTS

A Walk-Through Guide

All Clear 3—Listening and Speaking (advanced level) is the third in this best-selling series of conversationally-oriented texts. High-frequency American English idioms such as *cold feet,* and *make do* are presented in meaningful contexts to develop speaking, listening, and pronunciation skills. This text is appropriate for listening/speaking, pronunciation, and vocabulary courses.

- **Theme-based units** feature more contextualized listening activities.

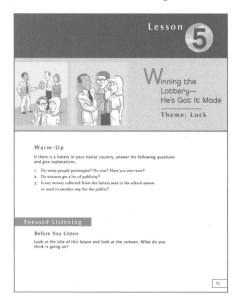

- **After You Listen** sections after each conversation increase comprehension.

- **Pronunciation** opportunities in every lesson to practice allow students to practice pronunciation in context.

- New **Internet**-based activities in every lesson relate to the lesson theme and give students the opportunity to apply content beyond the classroom.

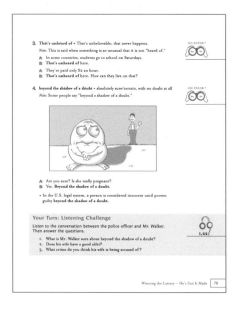

- **Your Turn** sections enhance comprehension by giving students the chance to personalize and connect idioms to their own lives and experiences.

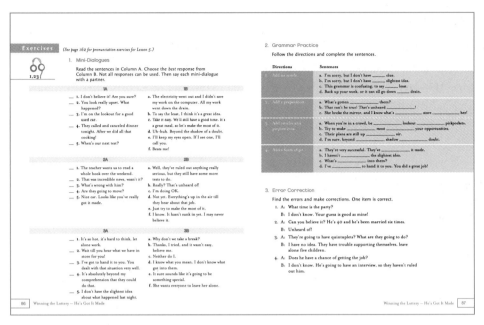

- **Grammar Practice** sections in every lesson teach students how to use idioms in complete, correct sentences.

- **Error Correction** sections provide editing practice.

- More **communicative activities** emphasize the practical uses of idioms in everyday conversations.

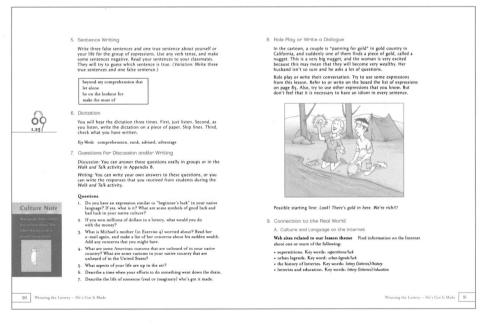

- Opportunities for role-playing, group work and delivering speeches, increase oral communication skills while meeting state standards.

- **Culture Note** boxes in every lesson apply the theme to the outside world and encourage discussion.

All Clear 3— Listening and Speaking is the new edition of *All Clear! Advanced.* Because the material in *All Clear 3* focuses on listening, speaking, pronunciation, culture, and public speaking in addition to idioms, this revised text would be appropriate in the following types of classes at the advanced level: listening/speaking, idioms, vocabulary, and pronunciation.

It was in the early 1980s when I wrote the first *All Clear,* which focused on idioms, and it is refreshing today to see such great interest in teaching with a lexical approach. While the initial focus of each lesson in this text is on lexical chunks of language (idioms and other expressions), students gain practice in all skill areas: listening, speaking, pronunciation, grammar, reading and writing.

It is well-known that in Listening/Speaking classes, it can be difficult to give homework and test and grade students because of the nature of the many open-ended activities. The inclusion of idioms in these classes brings in more concrete language material that can be easily assigned as homework and subsequently assessed.

All Clear 3

- exposes students to conversational situations that can serve as a basis for conversation practice, often with a cross-cultural focus.
- provides many structured and communicative activities for speaking, listening, grammar, writing, pronunciation and public speaking practice.
- teaches students to recognize and produce high-frequency idioms and expressions.
- contextualizes the study of pronunciation by integrating it with the study of idioms.

All Clear 3 starts with an Icebreaker activity, and is then divided into eight lessons, four review sections, a pronunciation section, and nine appendices.

The Icebreaker

To get to know each other, students mill around and ask each other questions based on information taken from student questionnaires completed in the previous class meeting. A sample questionnaire and sample *Find Someone Who . . .* activity are provided.

The Lessons

The lessons integrate listening, speaking, pronunciation, grammar, and writing, while focusing on teaching common expressions. Throughout each lesson, students are given opportunities to be very active and involved learners. Varied activities and numerous visuals are designed to reach students with a range of learning styles.

It is possible to move through the text in random order. Each lesson is independent, except in one area: pronunciation. If you plan to make pronunciation a substantial component of your course, you might prefer to follow the lessons in order because the pronunciation points build upon one another. The pronunciation part of each lesson appears in a separate section towards the back of the text.

You might want to start with Lesson I, as it has more detailed instructions than the other lessons.

Warm-Up

Students answer questions about their opinions or personal experience related to the lesson theme.

Culture Note

Culture Notes may appear at any point in a lesson.

Focused Listening

Before You Listen: Students look at a cartoon and try to guess what the characters are saying.

As You Listen: Students listen to a conversation with their books closed, and then answer two general questions about the main idea. They listen again as they read the conversation.

After You Listen: To check their comprehension of details, students do a *True/False* exercise. Then, by looking at paraphrases of five expressions, they try to guess meanings.

NEW!

Understanding the New Expressions

This section teaches the meanings, forms, and uses of expressions that appear in the introductory conversation.

- Meanings are revealed in explanations, mini-dialogues and example sentences.
- Related expressions (those that are similar or opposite in appearance and/or meaning) are included.
- Grammar and pronunciation notes call students' attention to details about expressions. Notes about usage are also included.
- *Your Turn* activities make this section interactive. Students immediately have opportunities to work with each other and use the new expressions.
- One *Your Turn: Listening Challenge* per lesson provides an additional listening opportunity.
- Origins of some idioms are given.
- Students evaluate their understanding of expressions by indicating whether or not the meanings are *all clear*.

NEW and INTERACTIVE!

Exercises

Students do exercises individually, in pairs, and in groups. When students work in groups, you might want to assign roles: leader, reporter, timekeeper, participant. Group leaders should make sure that students know each other's names, that everyone participates in a balanced way, and that the group stays on task and completes the activity at hand.

The ten exercises move from structured to communicative. (The exercises with an asterisk appear on the audio program.)

Focus on Form and Meaning

1. **Mini-Dialogues** (matching): In the mini-dialogues, students see the expressions in new contexts that help them understand the meanings of the expressions.*

NEW! 2. **Grammar Practice**: Given specific directions to use certain parts of speech or change verb tenses, students focus on form.

NEW! 3. **Error Correction** (one item is correct): Students continue to focus on form as they analyze sentences with errors.

4. **Choosing the Idiom** (fill-in): This exercise brings together what students have worked on in the preceding three exercises—recognizing which expression to use (meaning) and providing it in the proper grammatical form.*

NEW! 5. **Sentence Writing**: In this guessing game activity, students have the opportunity to use the new expressions in individual sentences.

6. **Dictation**: For more listening practice, students listen to a summary of the introductory conversation using reported speech. Key words are provided to help with spelling.*

Focus on Communication

7. **Questions for Discussion and/or Writing**: In this communicative exercise, students work in a small group or mill around and ask their classmates a variety of questions, some of which are based on the lesson theme, and some of which require the use of idioms. To make this a writing activity, students can write their own or other students' responses to the questions.

8. **Role Play or Write a Dialogue**: Students role play or write a dialogue based on a cartoon.

9. **Connection to the Real World**: This two-part exercise is the culmination of the entire lesson.

NEW! A. **Culture and Language on the Internet**: Students make speeches, participate in panel discussions, or listen to guest speakers. To find material for their presentations, students search websites related to the lesson theme or related to idioms, proverbs, quotations, urban legends, phrase origins, or euphemisms.

B. **Contact Assignment:** Students ask native English speakers to explain some phrasal verbs.

10. **Expression Collection:** Students keep an inventory of expressions heard outside of class.

Review Sections

After every two lessons, a "Collocation Match-Up" exercise and a crossword puzzle provide students with opportunities for review.

Pronunciation Section

This section, most of which focuses on suprasegmentals (stress, intonation and rhythm), appears towards the back of the text. This allows the teacher to introduce this material if time allows and at whatever time during a lesson that may be appropriate. The contexts of the pronunciation exercises come from every lesson, providing students with practice of meaning as well as pronunciation.

Appendices

Nine appendices provide support and supplementary material for the lessons. One new appendix contains speech instructions and feedback forms for teacher, peer, and self-evaluations. Other new appendices contain instructions for panel discussions and visits by guest speakers.

Audio Program

The audio program uses natural speech to present the following from each lesson:

- Introductory Conversation
- Listening Challenge
- Exercise 1—Mini-Dialogues
- Exercise 4—Choosing the Idiom
- Exercise 6—Dictation
- Pronunciation

I hope that you and your students enjoy using *All Clear 3,* and I welcome your comments and suggestions.

Helen Kalkstein Fragiadakis

Helen Kalkstein Fragiadakis
Contra Costa College
San Pablo, California

Dear Student,

Welcome to *All Clear 3 Listening and Speaking*. As you use this text and improve your listening and speaking skills, you will also learn idioms and other expressions that are so necessary for effective communication in English.

Listening and Speaking

In *All Clear 3,* you will have many opportunities to practice and develop your listening skills. As you listen to conversations, you will listen for main points and details. You will also have the opportunity to guess the meanings of new expressions from the contexts of the conversations. In dictations and pronunciation exercises, you will have additional listening practice.

As an advanced student, you would no doubt like to have numerous opportunities to speak in class. Many speaking opportunities are built into this text. You will have informal conversations in pairs and small groups, and also make formal individual and group presentations to your class. You will use the Internet to gather information on such topics as dating customs, homelessness and education.

About Idioms

As all students of a foreign language know, it is important to keep adding to your knowledge of vocabulary. You probably realize that when you don't understand what you hear, it is not always because someone is speaking too fast. It is often because you don't know some of the words or expressions being used.

As you work on increasing your vocabulary, it is best to not focus only on individual words because so much vocabulary comes in word groups—in phrases and expressions. Words that naturally go together are called *collocations.* When you learn more and more of these groups of words, you will find that your confidence will increase and that you will have the courage to use English more often.

In *All Clear 3,* the springboards for listening and discussion come from introductory conversations that contain numerous phrases and expressions. Some of these phrases and expressions are "idiomatic" and have special meanings. An example of an idiomatic expression is *once in a blue moon,* which means *not often* or *rarely.*

I've taught students at your level for many years, and have found that the following is what they need and want when studying idioms:

- to recognize and use the most common expressions
- to see numerous examples of the expressions in different contexts and in natural language
- to clarify how these expressions resemble or are different from other expressions they've heard
- to learn how to pronounce these expressions, not only alone, but also as parts of sentences
- to know the grammar associated with each expression
- to know any particular information about the use of expressions—for example, whether an expression is appropriate to say to a boss or a teacher as well as to a best friend
- to have a lot of opportunities to practice using the expressions in both speaking and writing

If you want to improve your listening and pronunciation skills, have meaningful discussions on topics that interest you, increase your vocabulary, and in general increase your confidence in your ability to use English, then our goals are the same.

Good luck to you, and I hope that you find the material in this text to be enjoyable and *all clear.*

Sincerely,

Helen Kalkstein Fragiadakis

Icebreaker

Directions

1. At the first class meeting, the students (and maybe also the teacher) should fill out the questionnaire below (or an adapted form).
2. At the second class, the students Walk and Talk, using the form on the next page. The questions students ask are based on their responses to the student questionnaire below.

STUDENT QUESTIONNAIRE

What is your name?   (Last)_____   (First) _____

What name do you want everyone to call you in class? _____

Where are you from? _____

What is your native language? _____

How long have you been in this English-speaking country? _____

OR

Have you ever been in a country where English is the main language?

___Yes   ___No

If yes, where? _____

What language or languages do you speak at home? _____

Do you work? _____

If yes, what do you do? _____

Are you a high school or college student?   ___Yes   ___No

If yes, what are you studying? _____

What do you like to do in your free time?

What is something interesting about you or someone in your family?

What do you want to learn in this class?

Is there anything that you would like to add? If yes, please write it here.

Walk and Talk

Stand up, get out of your seat, and get to know your classmates. Find out the information in this Walk and Talk activity by talking to at least five different students. The questions you ask are based on your responses on the student questionnaires.

Steps:

- Get up and ask a student the first question.
  If the student says "yes," then ask "What is your (first) name?" If necessary, also ask "How do you spell that?" Then write the student's first name on the line at the right. If a student says "no," say "Thanks anyway" and move on to another student.
- Continue until you have a name next to each question.
- After everyone is finished, your teacher can ask for the names of students who said 'yes' to each question and ask them for more information.

SAMPLE

Find Someone Who . . .	**First Name**
1. is from Mexico (Question: "Are you from Mexico?")	_____
2. speaks three languages	_____
3. speaks a little bit of English at home	_____
4. is a cook/manicurist/doctor/businessman/businesswoman	_____
5. plays the guitar	_____
6. has four sisters and five brothers	_____
7. speaks Japanese	_____
8. plans to get a degree in engineering	_____

At a Party—Taking the Initiative

Theme:
Meeting New People

Warm-Up

1. What do you prefer to do—go to a party or stay home and watch a movie? Why?
2. How do you feel at parties where you don't know many of the people?
3. When you want to start a conversation at a party with someone you don't know, what are some things you can talk about?

Focused Listening

Before You Listen

What do you think the men in the cartoon are saying to each other? What do you think the women are saying?

As You Listen

(A) Close your book. Listen to the conversation between Al and Bill to find the answers to these questions.

What does Bill want to do?   How does Al help his friend?

(B) Listen again, but this time read the conversation as you listen.

AL: **What's eating you?**

BILL: What do you mean? I'm fine.

AL: No, you aren't. Come on, whatever it is, **get it off your chest.**

BILL: Well . . . see that woman over there? Her name's Elizabeth. I've been trying to find a way to meet her for months, and now, here she is. But I don't **have the guts** to walk over there.

AL: Come on, Bill! This is your chance. Just **give it a shot.** What do you have to lose?

BILL: She **wouldn't be caught dead with me.**

AL: Why do you say that?

BILL: Oh, let's just **skip it,** OK? I don't know why I even told you.

AL: How do you know her, anyway?

BILL: We work in the same building.

AL: Well, I think you should just **bite the bullet,** go over there, and start a conversation.

BILL: Maybe later.

AL: Why **put it off?** Who knows? You two might **hit it off.**

BILL: **That'll be the day.**

AL: Why are you so negative all of a sudden? I've never seen you like this.

BILL: Maybe you're right. I should just **take the initiative** and walk over there. But what should I say?

AL: **Now you're talking.** Just introduce yourself and start talking about the party or mention that you've seen her at work. She's **bound to** recognize you, too.

BILL: Well, maybe. Oh . . . you're probably right. If I **pass up** this chance, I'll never forgive myself. Well, here I go. Wish me luck!

After You Listen

(A) Read the sentences about the conversation. Circle *T* for *true*, *F* for *false*, or *?* if you don't know.

1. This is the first time that Bill has seen Elizabeth.   T F ?
2. Bill has a lot of confidence in himself.   T F ?
3. Al offers to tell Elizabeth that Bill wants to meet her.   T F ?
4. Al gives Bill advice about what to say to Elizabeth.   T F ?
5. Al wants to meet Elizabeth's friend.   T F ?

Guess the Meanings

When you say the same thing with different words, you are paraphrasing. Read the paraphrases below, and find an expression in the conversation that means the same thing. Make sure the paraphrase would easily fit into the conversation.

Paraphrase   Idiomatic Expression

Example: *What's eating you?*   <u>What's bothering you?</u>

1. have the courage   _____

2. try it.   _____

3. (let's) not talk about it   _____

4. that will never happen   _____

5. don't take advantage of   _____

C Say the conversation in pairs. Then have two students say the conversation in front of the class.

Understanding the New Expressions

Work with Others

If you're working with a partner or in a small group, read the short dialogues and examples for each expression aloud. Also complete the Your Turn exercises together. Then, for each expression, circle *Yes* or *No* to show if you understand. If you circled *No*, highlight or underline what is unclear, and ask questions for clarification.

Figure It out on Your Own

Read the short dialogues and examples for each expression. Also complete the Your Turn exercises that don't need partners. Then, for each expression, circle *Yes* or *No* to show if you understand. If you circled *No*, highlight or underline what is still unclear, and ask questions in class for clarification.

1. **Whát's éating (you)?** = What's bothering you?

A: I don't want to talk right now.
B: **What's eating you?**
A: Nothing. I'll talk to you later.

A: **What's eating him** today? He's in a really bad mood.
B: I don't know. But let's stay out of his way until he feels better.

2. **gét something óff one's chést** = reveal something (usually a confession or complaint) that has been bothering you

A: I have to **get something off my chest.** It's been bothering me for a long time.
B: What is it?
(possible responses)
A: • I don't want you to borrow my car anymore because you put on so many miles. (confessing first and then complaining)
• I don't think it's fair that his salary is higher than mine. (complaining)
• I haven't been honest with you. (confessing)
• I lied to you. (confessing)

Contrast the Opposite:

kéep something bottled úp (inside) = keep something that has been bothering you inside.

A: It's not healthy to **keep** all those feelings/problems/thoughts **bottled up inside.** You can get sick. You need to talk to someone.

B: You're right. Can I talk to you?

Your Turn

Imagine that you are a famous actor. You are talking to another actor. Follow the directions and complete the sentences.

Actors' names: _____ and _____

Directions for A	Lines (What you and your partner say.)
Make a confession.	A: I have to *get something off my chest.* I _____. B: Really? _____!
Complain.	A: I have to *get something off my chest.* I'm upset because you _____. B: I'm sorry. I _____!
Give advice to someone who is very worried.	A: Tell me what's wrong. It's not good to *keep things bottled up.* B: OK. I _____.

3. **(nót) háve the gúts (to)** = (not) have the courage (to do something)

Note: When someone is afraid, it is common to use the expression *not have the guts.* The affirmative form is often used in questions.

A: Do you **have the guts to** swim there? There may be snakes.
B: No, I **don't have the guts.**
- She's scared. She **doesn't have the guts to** dive off that cliff.
- I don't **have the guts to** make a speech in front of the whole class.

4. **gíve it a shót** = try something; give something a chance to happen (while knowing you can make a change if it doesn't work out)

Note: Don't use this idiom with something that requires a long-term moral or ethical commitment such as marriage or getting a pet.

A: I was offered a new job.
B: Will you take it?
A: Yeah, I think I'll **give it a shot.** (= I'll try it, and if it isn't right for me, I'll look for another job.)

A: I don't know if we should move all the way across the country.
B: Maybe you should **give it a shot** for six months, and then decide on where to live.

1,2

Your Turn: Listening Challenge

Listen to Part A of the conversation. With your partner(s), come up with possibilities about what the two friends are talking about.

We think they might be talking about _____

_____

Now listen to Part B to see if you were correct.

5. **(someone) wóuldn't be cáught déad (with someone)** = someone would never want to be with someone because of dislike, fear, or shame

Note: This is a very, very strong expression that you should learn just for comprehension.

- You know, those two politicians **wouldn't be caught dead with each other**.
- She **wouldn't be caught dead with** those fanatics.
                                        her ex-boyfriend.

Contrast: **wouldn't be caught dead (in/at a place)**
          wouldn't be caught dead (do<u>ing</u> something)

- They **wouldn't be caught dead in** that part of town.
- We **wouldn't be caught dead at** that kind of concert.
- I **wouldn't be caught dead mak<u>ing</u>** a speech in front of a thousand people.

6. **Skíp it!** = Let's not talk about it anymore. = **Forgét it!**

Note: "Skip it!" and "Forget it!" are commands that are not very polite. They are used by very close friends or relatives when they don't want to answer a question.

A: Come on. Tell me what's wrong.
B: Let's just **skip it**, OK? I don't want to talk about it.

Contrast: **skíp something** = miss something on purpose, not by accident
          skíp lines = not write on every line; leave an empty space (line)
          skíp dessert = not eat dessert
          skíp over = intentionally not deal with a certain part of something
                        or with certain people:

- When I read the book, I **skipped over** the introduction.
- They **skipped over** us, and picked Rose and Rob to do the job.

ALL CLEAR ?

Yes No

7. **bíte the búllet (and do something)** = make a decision to do something after hesitating

Origin: During wars in the 1800s, doctors often had to cut off the arms or legs of soldiers. Because they didn't have medicine to help kill the pain, doctors gave soldiers a bullet to bite on. The meaning of *bite the bullet* is that a person makes a decision and does something with courage. (Source: *Morris Dictionary of Word and Phrase Origins*)

- Don't keep talking about it. Just **bite the bullet** and do it.
- They **bit the bullet** and got married.
- I'm going to **bite the bullet** and buy that new car.

Note: When you *bite the bullet,* you make a strong decision to DO something. When you *give something a shot,* you just try something and may or may not be successful.

ALL CLEAR ?

Yes No

8. **put something óff** = postpone, delay until later

A: You know the expression "Don't **put off** till tomorrow what you can do today?"
B: Uh-huh.
A: I do the opposite. I don't do today what I can do tomorrow. How about you?

Grammar Notes: **Put off** is a verb with two parts. It is called a *phrasal verb.*

(1) If you use a pronoun with this expression, be sure to put the pronoun *between* the two words.

A: I have a lot of homework this weekend.
B: Don't **put *it* off** for too long, or you'll be sorry.
    (**it** = homework)

(2) When a verb follows *put off,* it is necessary to add **-ing** to form a gerund:

- Don't **put off** do**ing** your homework.
- Doing your homework on time is important. Don't **put it off**.
  (Use "it" as the pronoun for a gerund.)
- He **put off** tell**ing** his boss about the problem, and now he's very nervous.

Your Turn

Procrastinators are people who delay doing things. Find three or four procrastinators in your class. Complete the chart.

ASK: Are you a procrastinator? Do you often put things off?

- When a classmate says "No, I never put things off," say "Thank you" and go talk to another student.
- When a classmate says "Yes," ask "What kinds of things do you often put off?"

Classmates who *put things off*	What they often *put off*
Example: 1. Andrea	1. She often puts off doing her laundry.

9. **hit it óff** = immediately get along with someone very well (This is said about people who meet for the first time and like each other very much.)

ALL CLEAR ?

Note: The word *hit* in this expression does not mean that someone actually hits or is hit.

Grammar Notes: The basic form of this expression doesn't change. The word *it* is always in the middle. However, the verb tense can change.

- When they met a few months ago, they **hit it off** right away, and now they see each other every day.
- I'm going to meet her parents tomorrow night. I hope we **hit it off**.
- We didn't **hit it off** very well, so I don't think we'll see each other again.

Your Turn

Discuss with a partner what qualities you like in another person. Then complete the dialogues.

A: How do you like your new roommate?

B: He's _____. We really *hit it off* and like each other a lot.

A: You joined an Internet dating service, didn't you?

B: Uh-huh. In fact, I went out with someone last week.

A: How was it?

B: Well, we didn't *hit it off*. I liked him/her on the phone, but _____

_____.

ALL CLEAR ?

10. **THÁT'LL be the dáy.** = That will never happen, in my opinion. This expression means "I don't expect that day to ever come."

Note: "That'll be the day" is a sarcastic expression because you are saying exactly the opposite of what you mean.

Pronunciation Note: Stress (give the most emphasis to) the word *That'll.*

A: Someday you'll be your own boss and you won't have to take orders from anyone.

B: **That'll be the day.**

A: They're trying to clean up the pollution here and plant more trees. Eventually our city will look like it did a hundred years ago.

B: **That'll be the day.**

Your Turn

What is something you don't believe will really happen? Complete the dialogue.

A: _____

B: That'll be the day!

11. **táke the inítiative (and do something)** = take the first step in doing something, take action (When you *take the initiative*, you don't wait for someone to tell you what to do.)

See Appendix I for a "Guide to pronunciation symbols."

Pronunciation Note: The *ti* in *initiative* is pronounced like *sh:* /ɪ-ní-ʃɪe-tɪv/.

A: She's very successful, isn't she?

B: She sure is. That's because she's not afraid to **take the initiative**. She doesn't hesitate to express her ideas and suggest projects.

- Nothing is going to happen if you don't **take the initiative**. You have to take the first step, because no one is going to come to you.
- You can **take the initiative** and:

    start something (a conversation, a business).

    ask someone out (for a date).

    suggest that something be done at work or in school.

    write a proposal for a project.

    make some phone calls to find something out.

12. **NÓW you're tálking.** = I didn't agree with what you said or were doing before, but now I completely and enthusiastically agree.

Pronunciation Note: Emphasize the word *now*. The point here is that I agree *now*, but I didn't agree before.

A: Let's take a week's vacation.

B: Only a week?

A: OK, a month.

B: **Now you're talking!**

A: You can have the car for $6,000.

B: Thanks anyway, but I think I'll look around.

A: How about $4,000?

B: **Now you're talking!** I'll take it.

13. **be bóund to** = be likely to; will probably

Grammar Note: This expression has a future meaning, but the verb *be* is used in the present tense.

- It's **bound to** rain. Look at the clouds.
- Don't worry about traveling there. Someone **is bound to** speak English.
- Your candidates **are bound to** win. They have a lot of money for advertising.
- She's **bound to** go out with you. After all, you're a great guy.

14. pass úp = to miss, not take advantage of an opportunity

Note: It is common to say *pass up an opportunity* or *pass up a chance* (to do something).

A: Can I take two weeks off?

B: When?

A: Soon. I won a free trip to Hawaii, and I have to use the ticket within thirty days. I don't want to **pass up** this great opportunity.

• You've got to say something now. It's the perfect time. Don't **pass up** this chance to talk to him.

Grammar Notes:

(1) Like **put off** (number 8), **pass up** is a phrasal verb. If you use a pronoun with this expression, be sure to put the pronoun *between* the two words:

• The dessert looks absolutely delicious. But I'm so full that I think I'll have to **pass *it* up.**

(2) When a verb follows *pass up*, it is necessary to add **-ing** to form a gerund:

• I don't want to **pass up** go***ing*** to Disneyland® for free!

Your Turn

Put a + next to what would be hard for you to *pass up*.
Put a – next to what wouldn't be hard for you to *pass up*.

Then talk to a partner and say:
It would/wouldn't be hard for me to pass up _____ because

_____.

___ ice cream

___ an all-you-can-eat buffet

___ a chance to adopt a cute puppy

___ free tickets to an opera

___ a big sale

___ a free trip to _____

___ _____

___ _____

NEW EXPRESSION COLLECTION

What's eating you?	wouldn't be caught dead	that'll be the day
get something off your chest	skip it	take the initiative
keep something bottled up	bite the bullet	now you're talking
(not) have the guts	put it off	be bound to
give it a shot	hit it off	pass up

(See page 150 for pronunciation exercises for Lesson 1.)

1. Mini-Dialogues

Read the sentences in Column A. Choose the *best* response from Column B. Not all responses can be used. Then say each mini-dialogue with a partner.

1,3

1A	1B
___ 1. There they are! It's our chance to get their autographs.	a. I've been keeping something bottled up for a long time.
___ 2. What's eating you?	b. Uh-huh. She bit the bullet and did it.
___ 3. Are you going to do it?	c. They wouldn't be caught dead there.
___ 4. They're parachute jumping today.	d. I know. I could never do that. I don't have the guts.
___ 5. Did she ask him out?	e. Let's go. I don't want to pass this up.
	f. Yup. I'm going to give it a shot.

Yup = Yes

2A	2B
___ 1. I think I'm going to skip it. I'm pretty tired.	a. What page?
___ 2. Skip over the first three paragraphs, and start with the fourth.	b. Tonight? Wow! They really put them off to the last minute.
___ 3. Look at how happy they are together.	c. Let's give it a shot.
___ 4. Don't call them. They're busy doing their taxes.	d. No problem there. I have a lot of ideas and the guts to try new things.
___ 5. We want someone for this job who isn't afraid of taking the initiative.	e. I don't see how you can pass this up.
	f. Yeah. I heard they hit it off right away.

2. Grammar Practice

Follow the directions and complete the sentences.

Directions	**Sentences**
I. Add an infinitive.	a. He doesn't have the guts _____*to talk*_____ to the teacher. b. You're bound _____ a lot if you see that comedy.
2. Add a gerund.	a. They wouldn't be caught dead _____ that mountain. b. I don't want to pass up _____ to L.A. c. Don't put off _____ your birthday.
3. Add an article.	a. Give it _____ shot! b. Bite _____ bullet! c. That'll be _____ day! d. Take _____ initiative!
4. Use past tense.	a. Yesterday I finally _____ something off my chest. I _____ the bullet and told my friend the truth. b. She _____ the initiative and started a conversation. They really _____ it off and fell in love. c. He _____ his feelings bottled up for a long time. He always _____ off telling her the truth.
5. Add a pronoun.	a. They put off their vacation. → They put _____ off. b. I passed up the cookies. → I passed _____ up.

3. Error Correction

Find the errors and make corrections. One item is correct.

1. I put off to do my laundry, and now I have nothing to wear.

2. A: Don't you have homework to do?

   B: Uh-huh. I'll do it later.

   A: Don't put off it. Do it now!

3. They met at a party last week and hitted it off.

4. If you want a new job, then take initiative and send your resume everywhere.

5. You bound understand more English if you learn a lot of idioms.

6. She doesn't want to pass it up this great opportunity.

7. She doesn't want to pass this opportunity up.

8. I wouldn't be caught dead to have a pet snake.

9. They didn't have the guts ski down that mountain.

10. At first, he was afraid to talk to her. But then he gave it shot.

4. Choosing the Idiom

You're watching a very emotional TV show with your friend. This is the conversation that you hear. Fill in the blanks with the best possible expressions from the list. Pay special attention to how the expressions are used grammatically. You may need to consider verb tenses, subject-verb agreement, pronouns, active vs. passive voice, etc. Not all of the expressions can be used. After you finish, practice reading the sentences aloud.

I,4

What's eating you?   get something off one's chest
(not) have the guts to   keep something bottled up inside
give it a shot   wouldn't be caught dead
hit it off   that'll be the day
put it off   bite the bullet
be bound to   pass up

JULIA: (1) _____ _What's eating you?_ _____ You look absolutely miserable.

JENNIE: Julia, I need some help. I've been offered the leading role in a big movie, but I (2) _____ say yes.

JULIA: Why not?

JENNIE: Oh, it's one of the actors. We worked on a movie together last year, and at first, we really (3) _____. But after a few weeks, I realized she was kind of crazy, and I told myself that I (4) _____ working with her ever again.

JULIA: And now you don't want to (5) _____ this chance to be a star?

JENNIE: You got it. What am I going to do? The movie (6) _____ be a big success. It's a great story, and the director is excellent.

JULIA: Why don't you talk to him? Tell him that you have something to (7) _____.

JENNIE: Yeah, right. I'm going to tell him that I won't work with his wife.

JULIA: His wife? This is getting really complicated.

JENNIE: I know I should (8) _____ and say something to him. And I can't (9) _____ any longer because he needs to know my decision. But what am I going to say? "Steven, I have to tell you that I want the part in the movie, but I can't work with your wife."

JULIA: (10) _____, and maybe he'll understand.

JENNIE: (11) _____!

5. Sentence Writing

Write three false sentences and one true sentence about yourself or your life for each group of expressions. Use any verb tense, and make some sentences negative. Read your sentences to your classmates. They will try to guess which sentence in each group is true. (*Variation:* Write three true sentences and one false sentence.)

Group 1	Group 2
keep things bottled up	put off
have the guts to	hit it off with …
wouldn't be caught dead	I said "That'll be the day" when …
pass up	take the initiative and …

After you read your sentences to your classmates, they can say, for example:
"I think it's true that you passed up the chance to go to a concert."

You can respond with:
"Yes, that's right. I passed up the chance to go to a concert."

OR

"No, that's wrong. I didn't pass up the chance to go to a concert."

I,5

6. Dictation

You will hear the dictation three times. First, just listen. Second, as you listen, write the dictation on a piece of paper. Skip lines. Third, check what you have written.

Key Words: bothering, admitted

7. Questions for Discussion and/or Writing

Discussion: Choose one of the activities below.

- Complete the *Walk and Talk* activity in Appendix B.
- In groups of three or four, answer the following discussion questions. Assign a discussion leader. The leader should make sure that everyone participates.

Writing: Choose one of the activities below.

- Write your own answers to the questions. Be sure to write complete sentences that contain the expressions in the questions.
- If you have done the *Walk and Talk* activity, write the responses of the students you talked to. Give their names and include the expressions that appear in the questions. To be sure that your sentences contain the correct information, you can *Walk and Talk* again and show your writing to the students who supplied the information.

Questions

1. Are you the kind of person who keeps things that bother you bottled up inside, or do you get things off your chest? Explain, and give some examples.

2. What are two activities or sports that scare you? Why don't you have the guts to do those things?

3. Do you generally do things on time, or do you put things off? Explain by giving some examples.

4. Have you ever hit it off with anyone immediately? Explain the circumstances.

5. What do you think life is bound to be like in fifty years?

6. What is one kind of food that you can never pass up?

7. What are two ways students can take the initiative to speak to native speakers of English?

8. Role Play or Write a Dialogue

In the cartoon, Katie is talking to her father about her job. She just found out that there is a two-year position open with her company in another country, and she is interested in applying. The problem is, she has no confidence in herself.

With a partner, role play or write the conversation between Katie and her father. Try to use some expressions from this lesson. Refer to or write on the board the list of expressions on page 12. Also, try to use other expressions that you know. But don't feel that it is necessary to have an idiom in every sentence.

Possible starting line: *So, how's work?*

9. Connection to the Real World

A. Culture and Language on the Internet

Web sites related to our lesson theme   Find information on the Internet about how to start a conversation. Key words: *conversation starters; small talk*. Or, find information about dating customs in different cultures.

Informally in a group or formally in a short speech, report back to your class on some specific new information that you learned.

Speech Instructions—
Appendix C

Idiom Web site   In this lesson, you learned the idiom, *What's eating you?* Here are some more expressions with *eat*. Find out what they mean from an idiom Web site. Key words: *idioms (+ the expression that you're looking up)*.

a bite to eat   have your cake and eat it too   eat like a bird

eat like a horse   eat your words

Phrase origin Web site   Find the origin of idioms and other expressions on the Internet. Key words: *phrase origins*. Choose one expression, explain it to your classmates, and give the origin of the expression.

B. Contact Assignment

In this lesson, you learned phrasal verbs with **pass** and **put**.

To learn more expressions with these words, with a partner ask a native speaker of English to help you fill out this chart. (For guidelines on how to do this kind of assignment, see Appendix F, "Contact Assignments," on page 197.)

		Meaning	Sample Sentence
pass			
	away	_____	_____
	back	_____	_____
	out	_____	_____
put			
	in for	_____	_____
	someone up	_____	_____

10. Expression Collection

Every week, find three expressions from the real world that are new to you. Keep an inventory in your notebook or on index cards, following the format in Appendix G, "Expression Collection," on page 198. Be ready to share what you found in small groups or with your entire class.

Kids' Behavior in Public— The Bottom Line

Theme: Behavior in Public

Warm-Up

How do you think children should behave in restaurants? On the left, write what they *should* do, and on the right, write what they *shouldn't* do. Then share what you have written with a partner or group.

In restaurants, children should . . .

_____

_____

_____

_____

In restaurants, children shouldn't . . .

_____

_____

_____

_____

Focused Listening

Before You Listen

Look at the cartoon above. What are two or three problems that you see?

As You Listen

(A) Close your book. Listen to the conversation to find the answers to these questions.

Why is the couple so upset? Give three reasons.
Who do you think is more upset—the couple or the waitress?

(B) Listen again, but this time read the conversation as you listen.

1,6

YIKES! = WOW!

WOMAN:	Yikes!
MAN:	What happened?
WOMAN:	I can't believe it! **All of a sudden,** a kid just ran in front of that waitress and she almost dropped her tray!
MAN:	What?
WOMAN:	Yeah, look! The parents are just sitting there while their kid's totally **out of control.**
MAN:	What? I can't hear you. It's so noisy in here.
WOMAN:	I said his parents aren't paying any attention to him **at all.** I don't think they **have a clue** that he's causing trouble.
MAN:	Well, this is just what we need after **going through all the trouble of** getting a babysitter. I thought we came here to eat **in peace for once.**
WOMAN:	Maybe we should just go somewhere else. It's **taking forever** to get our food anyway.
MAN:	That's not a bad idea.
WOMAN:	Uh-oh, it's too late. Our food's coming . . .
WAITRESS:	Sorry for the wait.
WOMAN:	That's OK. You're really busy tonight. I saw what just happened with that kid. You have a pretty dangerous job!
WAITRESS:	Yeah, unfortunately not all parents **keep** their kids **under control.** But I guess that's part of the job.
MAN:	Well, we'd never **put up with** that kind of behavior from *our* kids. I **have nothing against** taking kids to restaurants, but **the bottom line is that** kids need to learn how to behave, especially in public.
WOMAN:	Oh look—**here comes** the manager. I think he's going to talk to them. I wonder if he's going to ask them to leave!

After You Listen

(A) Read the sentences about the conversation. Circle *T* for *true*,
F for *false*, or *?* if you don't know.

1. The couple that is complaining has children.   T   F   ?
2. The man doesn't think children should
   be taken to restaurants.   T   F   ?
3. It took a long time for the food to arrive.   T   F   ?
4. The waitress hates her job.   T   F   ?
5. The manager is going to ask the couple
   with the boy to leave.   T   F   ?

(B) **Guess the Meanings**
Below is a list of paraphrases of five of the idiomatic expressions in the
conversation. On your own or with a partner, try to guess the five.

Paraphrase	Idiomatic Expression
1. without any warning	_____
2. tolerate	_____
3. the main point is that	_____
4. is taking a long time	_____
5. have any idea	_____

(C) Say the conversation in groups of three. Then have three students
say the conversation in front of the class.

Understanding the New Expressions

Work with Others

If you're working with a partner or in a small group, read the short
dialogues and examples for each expression aloud. Also, complete the
Your Turn exercises together. For each expression, circle *Yes* or *No* to
show if you understand. If you circled *No*, highlight or underline what is
unclear, and ask questions for clarification.

Figure It out on Your Own

Read the short dialogues and examples for each expression. Also
complete the Your Turn exercises that don't need partners. Then, for
each expression, circle *Yes* or *No* to show if you understand. If you circled
No, highlight or underline what is still unclear, and ask questions in class
for clarification.

1. **áll of a súdden** = suddenly, without warning

   - The room was very quiet, and then **all of a sudden,** everyone yelled "Surprise!"
   - We were just sitting down to dinner when **all of a sudden,** the earthquake hit.

2. **be óut of contról** = be disruptive, misbehave ≠ **be under control** (See Number 9.)

   - When the substitute teacher had the class, the kids **were out of control.** They were running around and throwing things, and the room was chaotic. But after the regular teacher returned, everything **was under control.**
   - The party **was out of control.** Strangers were coming in, the music was too loud, and some people were out yelling in the street. So someone called the police.

3. **(not) at áll** = zero percent

   Note: This expression is usually used at the end of negative statements. It emphasizes the idea of zero percent of something.

   - He **isn't** friendly **at all.** (He is 100 percent unfriendly.)
   - I did**n't** like that movie **at all.** (I disliked it 100 percent.)

   Similar Expression: **nothing at all (+ infinitive)** OR
   nothing (+ infinitive) **at all** = absolutely nothing (zero)

   - I've had **nothing at all** to eat today.
     OR
   - I've had **nothing** to eat **at all** today.
   - That has **nothing at all** to do with my point.
     OR
   - That has **nothing** to do with my point **at all.**

Your Turn

Ask a partner these questions.

1. What is something that you don't like at all? Why?
2. What is something about English that you don't understand at all? Why?
3. What is something that you don't want to do at all? Why?

4. **(not) have a clue (about** OR **that)** = (not) have any idea

Notes:

(1) A *clue* is a piece of information that helps solve a mystery or a problem.

(2) This expression is used to show that people don't know about something—either because they don't understand it, they don't realize it, or because they have no information about it.

Grammar Note: This expression is usually used in the negative form. However, it is also used in the affirmative after the phrase "I don't think ..."

1. **A:** I tried to listen to the lecture. But I do**n't have a clue** about what she said.
   B: Don't worry. When we have lunch, I'll explain everything to you.

2. **A:** Do you know what time we're supposed to meet them?
   B: I do**n't have a clue.**

3. **A:** I don't think he **has a clue** that she likes him.
   B: Should we tell him?

Your Turn

Look at the three mini-dialogues above with **have a clue.** Circle the dialogue number that fits each situation.

Situation	Dialogue Number		
1. He doesn't understand something.	I	2	3
2. He doesn't realize something.	I	2	3
3. He doesn't have any information about something.	I	2	3

5. **gó through (all) the troúble of** (+ gerund) = do something that is difficult or takes time, and then have disappointing results.

Grammar Note: Always use a gerund after 'of' with this expression.

A: I can't believe that I **went through the trouble of** arrang**ing** everything for the party, and then no one came!

B: I think that's because you put the wrong date on the invitation.

- After **going through the trouble of** cook**ing** all of his favorite kinds of food, she was unhappy that he didn't eat anything.
- She **went through the trouble of** cook**ing** all of his favorite kinds of food, but he didn't eat anything.
- He **went through the trouble of** help**ing** his brother with math for four hours, but his brother still failed his test.

Your Turn

With a partner, complete these sentences with a form of **go through the trouble of** (+ gerund). Follow the patterns of the three bulleted examples above.

1. After _____,
they didn't even thank her.

2. We _____,
but when we visited them, they didn't take us anywhere.

3. They _____
a babysitter for the kids, but they didn't have a good time and they wished they had just stayed home.

6. **in péace** = in a quiet atmosphere

Note: This expression is usually used when a person wants to leave a place that is noisy or chaotic.

- Come on. Let's get a cup of coffee. We need a place where we can talk **in peace**. It's just too noisy here.
- I'm going to the library. I need to study **in peace**.

Related Expression: **rest in peace**

This expression is used only when referring to someone who has died. People often say, "May s/he **rest in peace**."

ALL CLEAR ?
Yes No

7. **for ónce** = for one time, after a period of time of *not* doing something

Note: This expression is usually said in anger or frustration. **For once** follows a statement that indicates a habit or pattern. The statement with **for once**, often a suggestion or wish, indicates an idea for change.

Habit or pattern to change	*For once*—suggestion for change
I. We always eat in front of the TV. →	Let's eat at the table **for once.**
2. You make too many promises that you don't keep. →	**For once,** I wish you'd keep your promise.

ALL CLEAR ?
Yes No

8. **táke (someone) foréver** (+ infinitive) = take a very long time

A: Did you finish your report?
B: Yes, finally. It **took me forever.**

Grammar Note: When this expression is not at the end of a sentence, it is followed by an infinitive.

- **It takes forever to drive** to the city these days. I think I'll take the train.
- **It's taking** her **forever to do** that homework assignment. It's really hard.
- Sorry I'm late. **It took** (me) **forever to get** out of the office.

Your Turn

Ask a partner these questions.

1. What is one thing that usually takes you forever to do? Why?

2. What is one thing that took you forever to do? Why?

3. What is one thing that you don't want to do because it will take you forever? Why?

9. **kéep (someone) under contról** = keep/maintain order

   - There's always a big crowd downtown on New Year's Eve. So there are a lot of police to **keep everyone under control.**
   - The new teacher couldn't **keep the kids under control,** so she went home and cried.

   Similar Expression:

   be under contról = be calm, organized, in order

   A: How are the kids? Are they driving you crazy?
   B: No, they're fine. Don't worry. Everything **is under control.**

   - After the earthquake, there wasn't much damage. No one panicked. Everything **was under control.**

10. **put úp with** (+ noun or gerund) = tolerate

   A: I know you like living in the city. But how can you **put up with** all the noise and the traffic?
   B: It doesn't bother me. For me, it's better than living in the quiet suburbs.

   - Tom and Angela won't **put up with** bad behavior. They punish their kids when they break the rules, but they don't hit them.
   - I won't **put up with** lying. Tell me the truth!

Your Turn

Sam is a teacher. Look at the list of things he can't or won't put up with. Then imagine what actions he will take for each item on the list.

What Sam can't/won't put up with	What Sam will do
1. cheating on tests	_____
2. students turning in their homework late	_____
	_____
3. teaching in a classroom that doesn't have enough heat	_____
	_____

11. **have nóthing against** (+ noun or gerund), **but . . .** = have no problem with, have no negative feelings about, but . . .

- He told me he **has nothing against** my best friend, **but** he doesn't like spending a lot of time with her.
- I **have nothing against** study**ing** in groups, **but** I'd rather study alone.

12. **the bóttom líne (is that . . .)** **=** the basic truth, the main point (is that . . .)

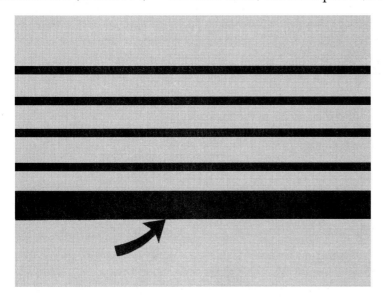

Origin: This expression originally related to profits and losses in business.

- I know you want to show me the details about the budget. But first, I want to know **the bottom line.** How much money did we lose last year?
- I know you're a vegetarian. I know you eat only organic foods. I know you get enough sleep. I know you take vitamins. But **the bottom line** is that you've got to exercise regularly.

Your Turn: Listening Challenge

Listen to the two situations. After each, complete the sentences below. Different answers are possible.

1,7

Situation 1
The bottom line is that

_____.

Situation 2
The bottom line is that

_____.

13. **hére cóme(s)** (name of someone) OR **here** (pronoun) **come(s)**

Note: This expression is always in the present tense.

- Look! **Here comes** Mike. Let's go say hello to him.
- Look! **Here come** Mike and Jan. Maybe they'll want to join us.
- OK. You've got to talk to her now. **Here she comes.**

A: If they don't come in five minutes, I think we should order our food.

B: Oh! I think I see them. Yes, **here they come.**

NEW EXPRESSION COLLECTION

all of a sudden	in peace	put up with
be out of control	for once	have nothing against
(not) at all	take forever	the bottom line
(not) have a clue	keep under control	here come(s)
go through the trouble of	be under control	

1. Mini-Dialogues

Read the sentences in Column A. Choose the *best* response from Column B. Not all responses can be used. Then say each mini-dialogue with a partner.

1,8

1A	1B
___ **1.** I don't know where Laura is.	**a.** I liked it, but my friend didn't like it at all.
___ **2.** I work 40 hours a week, but I hardly make any money.	**b.** So what did you do?
___ **3.** How did you like that new restaurant?	**c.** I don't have a clue.
___ **4.** You've had nothing at all to eat. Are you OK?	**d.** Let's help everyone calm down. We need to keep everyone and everything under control.
___ **5.** Where do they live?	**e.** Look! Here she comes!
___ **6.** I couldn't believe it! All of a sudden, he started crying.	**f.** I think so. I just don't have an appetite right now.
	g. Well, the bottom line is that you need to get more education so you can get a better job.

2A	2B
___ **1.** We went through the trouble of arranging for them to meet, but neither of them wanted to come.	**a.** To the library. I need to study in peace.
___ **2.** Where are you going?	**b.** Because it's too expensive. You know that!
___ **3.** We always go camping. Why don't we stay at a hotel for once?	**c.** It's hard, but I have no choice.
___ **4.** Is he OK?	**d.** I'll get their parents.
___ **5.** How do you put up with all that noise upstairs?	**e.** I didn't understand him at all.
___ **6.** Why don't you want to come to the concert? You know I have free tickets.	**f.** Yeah, he's fine. It took me forever to reach him because of the storm, but finally I got through.
___ **7.** These kids are out of control. They're driving me nuts!	**g.** So what did you do?
	h. I know, and I don't have anything against classical music. But it always puts me to sleep.

2. Grammar Practice

Follow the directions and complete the sentences.

Directions	Sentences
1. Add an article.	a. All of _____ sudden, the alarm went off. b. We're planning a surprise party for him, and he doesn't have _____ clue. c. _____ bottom line is that nothing is forever and we have to appreciate each day.
2. Add a preposition.	a. I don't want to go through the trouble _____ doing all this research for nothing. b. The police came because the crowd was out _____ control. c. I don't understand why you did that _____ all. d. All _____ a sudden, she got up and left the room. e. I don't have a clue _____ what she was talking about. f. She has no problem putting up _____ all the mess in her house. She's very relaxed about it. g. You always drive. _____ once, I'd like to drive. h. I don't mind dogs. I have nothing _____ them. But I would never have one. i. The babysitter made sure that everything was _____ control before the parents returned. j. I need to do my work _____ peace. Can you please close the door?
3. Add an infinitive.	a. We stayed in a boring little town. There was nothing at all _____ on Saturday night. b. It took him forever _____ how to use that new computer program.
4. Add a gerund.	a. I went through the trouble of _____ everyone's e-mail address, and then I lost the list! b. How can you put up with _____ here? It's so noisy and polluted! c. He has nothing against students _____ their native languages with each other. But he doesn't want them to do that in class.

3. Error Correction

Find the errors and make corrections. One item is correct.

1. All of the sudden, the lights went out.
2. It took forever to cook this, but it's delicious.
3. She doesn't have nothing against using email, but she'd rather write letters.
4. Bottom line is that life is short.
5. Look! Here come Bill!
6. Look! Here Bill comes!
7. Look! Here they came!
8. I'm so confused. I don't have a clue on what the teacher said today.
9. He went through the trouble of get ready for the picnic, but then it rained.
10. We liked the concert at all.

4. Choosing the Idiom

Jim and Julie, the couple in the booth from page 19, are driving home and talking about what happened in the restaurant. Fill in the blanks with the best possible expressions from the list. Pay special attention to how the expressions are used grammatically. You may need to consider verb tenses, subject-verb agreement, pronouns, active vs. passive voice, etc. Not all of the expressions can be used. After you finish, practice reading the sentences aloud.

1,9

the bottom line is that
all of a sudden
under control
in peace

not have a clue that
go through the trouble of
at all
put up with

JULIE: I am *so* embarrassed. I don't want to ever go back there again.

JIM: Neither do I. When we couldn't get a babysitter, we should've just stayed home.

JULIE: You know, I was shocked. One minute we were enjoying our dinner, and then

(1) _____ the

manager was asking us to leave. I can't believe it.

JIM: Well, it's true that we weren't paying any attention to Davy. We weren't keeping Davy

(2) _____ and

he got into trouble. It's our fault.

JULIE: But the manager wasn't polite (3) _____.

Can you believe that he said that people wanted to eat (4) _____

_____ and that we were making that

impossible? I (5) _____

Davy was a problem.

JIM: Well, you have to admit that we weren't looking. I understand that he was getting in

the way. We're lucky that the waitress didn't drop her tray on him!

JULIE: Hmm. That's for sure! Actually, I remember when I was a waitress and we had to

(6) _____

little kids. I almost spilled coffee on a kid once.

JIM: You never told me that!

JULIE: I forgot about it till now. I guess the manager was right. (7) _____

_____

it's not safe when kids run around a restaurant. I'm so embarrassed!

5. Sentence Writing

Write three false sentences and one true sentence about yourself or your life for each group of expressions. Use any verb tense, and make some sentences negative. Read your sentences to your classmates. They will try to guess which sentence in each group is true. (*Variation:* Write three true sentences and one false sentence.)

Group 1	**Group 2**
all of a sudden	go through the trouble of
at all	for once
nothing at all	take forever
not have a clue about	put up with

6. Dictation

You will hear the dictation three times. First, just listen. Second, as you listen, write the dictation on a piece of paper. Skip lines. Third, check what you have written.

1,10

Key Words: behavior, waitress

7. Questions for Discussion and/or Writing

Discussion: You can answer these questions orally in groups or in the *Walk and Talk* activity in Appendix B.

Writing: You can write your own answers to these questions, or you can write the responses that you received from students during the *Walk and Talk* activity.

Culture Note

In the United States, it is illegal for teachers to hit children in school as a way to punish them. What are the rules or laws about punishment in schools in your native country?

Questions

1. In your native culture, is it common for parents to take children to restaurants? How common is it to get a babysitter?

2. In your native culture, how do parents punish their children?

3. When you are disturbed by noise at a restaurant or movie theater, what do you do? (a) Nothing? (b) Talk directly to the people who are bothering you? (c) Talk to the manager? Explain.

4. What do you do when someone near you at a restaurant or movie theater is talking on a cell phone? Do you have your cell phone on when you're in restaurants or theaters? If yes, do you think about how loud you are talking?

5. What can't you put up with in the following places? (a) at school (b) at home (c) in a store (d) in a restaurant (e) in a theater (f) in a bus (g) on a train or plane

6. What is one part of the world that you don't have a clue about?

7. What are some places where you can read, relax, or study in peace?

8. Do you think it will take forever to learn enough English? Why or why not?

8. Role Play or Write a Dialogue

In the cartoon, Greg and Melissa are at a restaurant and someone at the next table is having a very loud conversation on his cell phone.

With a partner, role play or write the conversation between Greg and Melissa. Try to use some expressions from this lesson. Refer to or write on the board the list of expressions on page 28. Also, try to use other expressions that you know. But don't feel that it is necessary to have an idiom in every sentence.

Possible starting line: *Wow! It was so quiet before and now I can't even hear myself think!*

9. Connection to the Real World

A. Culture and Language on the Internet

Web sites related to our lesson theme   Find information on the Internet about any of the following:

Topics	**Possible Key Words**
1. children's behavior in public	children/restaurants/behavior
2. cell phones in public	cell phone etiquette
3. movie theater behavior	movie theater etiquette
4. types of punishment for children	corporal punishment

- Informally in a group or formally in a short speech, report back to your class on some specific new information that you learned.

OR

- Participate in a panel discussion about one or both of the following topics:

(1) Various kinds of etiquette. Search the Internet with the key words "Miss Manners/etiquette." Divide the information you gather among panel members.

(2) Corporal punishment at home and/or at school. Possible roles for panel members: child psychologist, doctor, teacher, mother, father, teenager, police officer

OR

- If you are at a school where there is a psychology or education department, invite an instructor or student from that department to talk to your class about types of punishment that are used to discipline children. Listen, take notes, and ask the speaker questions.

Idiom Web site   Find the meanings of these idioms with the word "once" on the Internet: *at once, once again, once and for all.* Share what you find with a partner.

> Speech Instructions—
> Appendix C

> Panel Discussion—
> Appendix D

> Guest Speaker—
> Appendix E

B. Contact Assignment

In this lesson, you learned the phrasal verb **put up with**.

To learn more expressions with **put,** with a partner ask a native speaker of English to help you fill out this chart. (For guidelines on how to do this kind of assignment, see Appendix F, "Contact Assignments," on page 197.)

Pronunciation Note: Remember to stress the second part of phrasal verbs.

	Meaning	**Sample Sentence**
put		
away	_____	_____
someone down	_____	_____
someone out	_____	_____
someone on	_____	_____

10. Expression Collection

Every week, find three expressions from the real world that are new to you. Keep an inventory in your notebook or on index cards, following the format in Appendix G, "Expression Collection," on page 198. Be ready to share what you found in small groups or with your entire class.

Collocation Match-Up

Collocations are special combinations of words. Collocations can be idioms or other phrases and expressions. Find collocations *from Lessons 1 and 2* by matching the words from Column A with words in Column B. Sometimes more than one answer is possible. (You will probably be able to make additional expressions that are not from Lessons 1 and 2. Put these in the box.)

A		**B**
1. have nothing	_against_	to
2. all of	_____	control
3. keep someone	_____	off
4. in	_____	off
5. take	_____	up with
6. be out of	_____	up
7. be bound	_____	up
8. the bottom	_____	forever
9. here she	_____	over
10. skip	_____	against √
11. skip	_____	clue
12. bite	_____	peace
13. put	_____	comes
14. put	_____	planning
15. pass	_____	under control
16. nothing	_____	line
17. be bottled	_____	it
18. hit it	_____	at all
19. not have a	_____	the bullet
20. go through the trouble of	_____	a sudden

Additional Collocations

Crossword Puzzle

Across

1   She ___ up with him because she loves him.

5   He said he wouldn't be ___ dead listening to that music.

6   After going through the ___ of driving up to the mountains in the rain, he got sick, so he spent his whole vacation in bed.

7   Don't wait for things to happen to you. Take the ___.

9   I don't have a ___ where they went.

11 For ___, let me make dinner. You go relax.

13 The ___ line is that idioms are really common, so we need to learn them.

14 All of a ___, they started singing.

15 Do you have the ___ to do it? I think it's scary.

Down

2   Give it a ___. You might be surprised to see that you'll do fine.

3   Now you're ___. I agree with you 100 percent.

4   This puzzle is taking me ___.

8   We didn't like that show at ___.

10 You don't look very happy today. What's ___ you?

12 Come on, tell me. Get it off your ___.

In Class—Bored to Death or on the Edge of Your Seat?

Theme:
School Life

Warm-Up

Complete the chart. On the left, list two things that would make a class boring. On the right, list two things that would make a class interesting.

Boring

_____

_____

Interesting

_____

_____

Before You Listen

Look at the title of this lesson and look at the cartoon. What do you think the two students are saying to each other?

As You Listen

(A) Close your book. Listen to the conversation between students Jan and Steve to find the answers to these questions.

Why is Jan bored in her class?
Why is Steve interested in his class?

(B) Listen again, but this time read the conversation as you listen.

JAN:	Mmm. This coffee is really strong.
STEVE:	I like it that way.
JAN:	So do I. All during my last class I was thinking about coming here and could almost taste the coffee.
STEVE:	Sounds like it wasn't too exciting.
JAN:	I was **bored to death.** I'm in that class only because it's a requirement, so I have to **stick it out.** The problem is, the professor doesn't know how to **spark our interest.** She just walks in and lectures. There's no discussion.
STEVE:	**What a drag!** Don't people ask questions?
JAN:	Oh, yeah, **once in a blue moon.** But I always see **an awful lot of** people doodling,* and I can tell their **minds are wandering.** Do you have any classes like that?
STEVE:	I have only one big lecture class—world history—and the professor's the best. It's so interesting, I'm always **on the edge of my seat.** And when we have discussions, the room is filled with electricity.
JAN:	I'm jealous. Too bad I already took world history.
STEVE:	You know, one day **it dawned on me** that I was lucky to be in her class because I found myself thinking a lot about what she said. Did you ever have a teacher like that?

Drawing pictures in their notebooks.

JAN: I'd have to think about it. I don't know.

STEVE: You should come with me to class sometime, just to see what I mean.

JAN: Sounds like you're in love with her, Steve.

STEVE: Very funny. She could be my grandmother. Anyway, I guess **what it really comes down to is** her enthusiasm for the subject. She just loves history. I remember at the beginning of the semester, I was **fooling around** a lot and not taking anything in school very seriously. I **bombed** the first history test, but then I **buckled down** because I started really enjoying school, especially her class.

JAN: You've got me really curious about this teacher. I think I'll **take you up on** your idea to visit your class. When does it meet?

After You Listen

(A) Below are details about the introductory conversation. Circle *T* for *true, F* for *false,* or *?* if you don't know.

1. Jan is staying in her class because it's too late to drop it.   T   F   ?
2. Jan's professor does most of the talking.   T   F   ?
3. Steve is going to take a class with Jan's professor next semester.   T   F   ?
4. Steve was lazy at the beginning of the semester.   T   F   ?
5. Students do less talking in Steve's class than in Jan's class.   T   F   ?

(B) **Guess the Meanings**
Below is a list of paraphrases of five of the idiomatic expressions in the conversation. On your own or with a partner, try to guess the five.

Paraphrase   Idiomatic Expression

1. How boring!   _____

2. failed   _____

3. accept   _____

4. I suddenly realized   _____

5. very rarely   _____

(C) Say the conversation in pairs. Then have two students say the conversation in front of the class.

Work with Others

If you're working with a partner or in a small group, read the short dialogues and examples for each expression aloud. Also complete the Your Turn exercises together. For each expression, circle *Yes* or *No* to show if you understand. If you circled *No*, highlight or underline what is unclear, and ask questions for clarification.

Figure It out on Your Own

Read the short dialogues and examples for each expression. Also complete the Your Turn exercises that don't need partners. Then, for each expression, circle *Yes* or *No* to show if you understand. If you circled *No*, highlight or underline what is still unclear, and ask questions in class for clarification.

ALL CLEAR ?

1. **be bóred to déath** = **be bóred stíff** = **be bóred to téars** = be extremely bored

    A: How was the movie?

    B: I **was bored to death.**

    A: The movie was three hours long and we **were bored stiff (bored to tears).**

    B: Why didn't you walk out?

    A: 'Cause everyone else wanted to stay till the end.

    Grammar Notes:

    (1) Only a *person* can be bored by something. (A movie can't be bored. It can be boring.)

    (2) This expression is often used in the passive voice (with the *-ed* past participle—*bored*).

Cause	Effect
(Events, things, or people are *boring*.)	(People are *bored*.)
The party is so boring! →	I agree. I'm bored to death. Let's go.
The book was boring. →	She was bored stiff so she fell asleep.
They're so boring! And they talked for hours! →	We were bored to tears.

Your Turn

Have you ever been bored to death by any of the following? If yes, tell your partner(s) about the specific situation.

- a movie
- a sports event
- a long speech
- a book that you had to read for school
- Other: _____

- a terrible party
- a terrible job
- a very long trip
- someone who talked too much
- _____

2. **stick it óut** = continue with something to the end, even if there are problems

   Grammar Note: You can change the verb tense in this expression, but you can't change the pronoun. Always use "it:" *stick it out, stuck it out, will stick it out,* etc.

   A: How are the winters in Alaska?
   B: Pretty tough. But we'll **stick it out** here for another two years.

   A: Come on, don't quit. You have only one more year of school.
   B: But I don't know if I can **stick it out**.

   - It was a difficult marriage. They **stuck it out** until their children were out of the house, but then they got a divorce.

   Contrast: **stick óut** = be especially visible in contrast to what is around

   A: What's that **sticking out of** your book?
   B: Oh—it's a twenty-dollar bill! I'm glad you saw it.

   - Your shirt is **sticking out.** Tuck it in.
   - Most people don't want to **stick out** in a crowd because they don't want to attract attention.

ALL CLEAR ?

Culture Note

The Japanese proverb, "the nail that sticks out gets hammered down" means that it is best for people to conform and be like others. Do you have a similar proverb in your native culture?

3. **spárk (someone's) ínterest (in)** = create an unusual amount of interest (in something)

   Note: A *spark* is a small, burning particle that is in a fire. It can blow in the wind and create another fire.

ALL CLEAR ?

A: Did you finish the book?

B: You know, I really couldn't get into it. I tried, but somehow the topic didn't **spark my interest.**

• His teacher **sparked his interest in** space travel. That's all he talks about now.

• His teacher **sparked his interest in** learning about space travel.

ALL CLEAR ?

Yes   No

4. **Whát a drág!** = That's terrible! That's too bad! How boring!

Note: This expression is very informal, and its definition depends on the context of the conversation.

A: After their car stereo was stolen, their house was robbed.

B: **What a drag!**

A: Yesterday I had two tests, today I have one, and tomorrow I have three.

B: **What a drag!**

A: I have to attend a meeting all day on Monday.

B: **What a drag!**

Your Turn

Complete the dialogue with a sentence about something bad or boring. Then read Part A to three students. Each student should respond with *What a drag!*

A: _____

B: *What a drag!*

5. ónce in a blúe móon = very rarely; not often

Note: This expression is very informal.

A: Do you ever hear from them anymore?
B: Once in a blue moon.

A: You work so much. Don't you ever get a day off?
B: Once in a blue moon.

ALL CLEAR ?

Origin: When a full moon occurs twice in a calendar month, the second moon is called a blue moon. This occurs very rarely.

Your Turn

Ask three students the following:
What is something that you do only once in a blue moon? Why?

6. an áwful lót (of) = a lot of; many/much

ALL CLEAR ?
Yes   No

Note: This expression is said for emphasis. It has nothing to do with the word *awful,* which has negative connotations.

- **An awful lot of** people were at the party.
- She made **an awful lot of** money in the stock market.
- He doesn't eat **an awful lot** (of food), but he's a big guy.

Contrast: At the end of a sentence, **an awful lot** without "of" means "frequently" or "often."

- They go to parties **an awful lot.**
- That teacher gives tests **an awful lot.**

Your Turn

Complete the chart about yourself and your partner.

	You	Your Partner
1. If you could have one of these, which would you choose and why? *(an awful lot of = much)* • an awful lot of money • an awful lot of friends • an awful lot of free time		
2. If you could do one of these, which would you choose and why? *(an awful lot = often)* • travel an awful lot • go to parties an awful lot • get exercise an awful lot		

7. **someone's mínd is wándering** = Someone is not paying attention and is thinking about different things.

Note: To *wander,* literally, is to walk around with no particular destination. When your mind wanders, it goes from one thought to another.

Pronunciation Note: Don't confuse the word *wonder* with *wander.* The *o* in *wonder* is pronounced like the *u* in the word *up.* The *a* in *wander* is pronounced like the *o* in the word *on.*

A: Jan, I asked you a question. Didn't you hear me?
B: I'm sorry. My **mind was wandering.**
A: I know. You should be paying attention.

- I was reading my book, but then I realized that **my mind was wandering** and I didn't remember anything I had read.
- My mind **wanders** every time I listen to him talk because he goes on and on.

Contrast: **wander aróund (a place)** = walk around with no particular destination

- We **wandered around** the city for three hours. It was great.
- I think I'll **wander around** the museum for a while. Why don't we plan to meet at the station at 2:00?
- It doesn't matter where we go. Let's just **wander around.**

8. be on the édge of one's séat = be extremely interested in something

Note: This is said when listening to or watching something.

ALL CLEAR ?
Yes No

- I **was on the edge of my seat** during the whole movie. And I was biting my nails.
- She **was on the edge of her seat,** listening attentively to every single word he said.

Your Turn

Think about a very competitive sports event or a very suspenseful movie when you were on the edge of your seat. Complete this sentence and tell a partner about your experience.

I was on the edge of my seat when . . . because . . . .

9. it dáwned on someone (who, what, where, when, why, how, how much, how many, that) = Someone suddenly thought of something.

ALL CLEAR ?
Yes No

Note: Dawn is the time of morning when the sun rises, when there is the beginning of light in the sky. When something *dawned on you,* some knowledge suddenly appeared out of the darkness.

Grammar Note: This expression usually occurs in the past tense.

- While I was reading the murder mystery, in the middle of chapter 6, **it dawned on me who** did it.
- She was on the train when **it** suddenly **dawned on her what** she'd done. She immediately went back home and apologized to her husband.
- I was in the shower when **it dawned on me where** I had put all the money.

- In the middle of the night **it dawned on** the police officer **when** the guy had had the chance to commit the murders.
- At first I didn't understand, and then **it dawned on me why** you said that.
- Then **it dawned on him how** she stole the money. It was late at night, . . .
- When he saw her face, **it dawned on him how much** she cared.
- **It dawned on her how many** times the truth was right there in front of her, but she didn't see it.
- Last night **it dawned on them that** they needed to do something—fast.

ALL CLEAR ?

10. **Whát it cómes dówn to is . . . = What it boils dówn to is . . . =** The main point/the bottom line* is . . .

Note: This is said when there is a longer explanation, but you want to say just your main point. Think of boiling a sauce. Much of the liquid evaporates, but the main or most important part stays.

- I know you care a lot about your education. But **what it comes down to (what it boils down to) is** that you have to work hard to succeed.

A: The police think he did it.
B: Why?
A: **What it comes down to is** that he had a motive and was near the scene of the crime.

A: She said she'd like to give me the job, but she can't.
B: Why not?
A: **What it boils down to is** my lack of experience.

ALL CLEAR ?

11. **fool aróund (with/in)** = do nothing constructive or nothing in particular; play

- The two children were **fooling around in** the back of the classroom, and the teacher told them to pay attention.

A: What did you do during the summer?
B: Nothing much, I just **fooled around with** my friends.
A: What did you guys do?
B: Oh, we went to the movies and the beach. Slept a lot.

For information on the bottom line, see Lesson 2.

12. **bómb (a test)** = **flunk** (a test) = fail (a test)

ALL CLEAR ?

Yes No

- I didn't study, so I **bombed** my test.
- After she **flunked** the test, she went to the tutoring lab to get help.

13. **buckle dówn** = start to work seriously

ALL CLEAR ?

Yes No

A: You've been fooling around long enough. Now it's time to **buckle down** and get to work if you want to learn something.

B: You're right. Starting right this minute, I''m off to a new start.

Contrast: **buckle úp** = put on a seat belt

- I want everyone in the car to **buckle up** before we start, OK?

14. **táke someone úp on something** = accept an invitation or an offer

ALL CLEAR ?

Yes No

A: How about dinner tonight, and then a movie?
B: That sounds great. I think I'll **take you up on** that.

A: Where's Jan?
B: Steve offered to take her to his history class, and she **took him up on** it.

Your Turn: Listening Challenge

First, listen to only Part A of the conversation. Then, with a partner, come up with possibilities about why the guy doesn't want to go to the party. To find out why he won't go, listen to Part B.

We think he doesn't want to go to the party because _____

I,12

NEW EXPRESSION COLLECTION

bored to death	an awful lot	what it boils down to
stick it out	my mind is wandering	fool around
stick out	wander around	bombed
spark interest	on the edge of my seat	buckle down
What a drag!	it dawned on me	buckle up
once in a blue moon	what it comes down to	take you up on

1. Mini-Dialogues

Read the sentences in Column A. Choose the *best* response from Column B. Not all responses can be used. Then say each mini-dialogue with a partner.

1,13

1A	1B
___ **1.** How often do you read a book?	**a.** What a drag!
___ **2.** I spent all weekend cleaning my apartment.	**b.** It sure was—I was on the edge of my seat for two hours.
___ **3.** Was the movie scary?	**c.** No, I don't. I work hard.
___ **4.** What was his speech about?	**d.** Once in a blue moon.
___ **5.** What it boils down to is that you fool around too much.	**e.** I'll take you up on that.
	f. I have no idea. My mind was wandering while he was speaking.

2A	2B
___ **1.** Come on. Can't you stay just one more hour?	**a.** Maybe *you* can stick it out, but *I* can't.
___ **2.** An awful lot of people want to get into this movie.	**b.** We all need to buckle up.
___ **3.** What sparked your interest in learning English?	**c.** A lot of people were bored to death, but I loved it.
___ **4.** How was the show?	**d.** No problem. Next time.
___ **5.** I'm sorry I can't take you up on your invitation.	**e.** Movies, I guess.
	f. I know—everyone is curious.

3A	3B
___ **1.** It just dawned on me that we can try to get that information on the Internet.	**a.** I know. Isn't it great? They decided to buckle down and work hard.
___ **2.** It comes down to this: either do the job or quit.	**b.** Yeah. It's a long story, but it boils down to one thing.
___ **3.** They were so lazy before. They've really changed.	**c.** It's sticking out.
___ **4.** What did you do when you got there?	**d.** We wandered around for a while, and then went out to dinner.
___ **5.** Did you find out what happened?	**e.** You're right. I need the money, so my decision is clear.
	f. You're right. Of course we can!

2. Grammar Practice

Follow the directions and complete the sentences.

Directions	Sentences
1. Add an article.	a. What _____ drag! We missed the movie! b. We eat out once in _____ blue moon. c. I like studying idioms _____ awful lot.
2. Add a preposition.	a. That book sparked my interest _____ art history. b. We wandered _____ the city for a while, and then we went to lunch. c. I was so scared that I was _____ the edge _____ my seat during the whole movie. d. It dawned _____ us that we needed to buy a gift. e. What it comes down _____ is that we need to get more exercise. f. I'm not using a recipe. I'm just fooling around _____ some interesting ingredients. g. The kids are fooling around _____ the backyard. h. If you really want to help, I'd be happy to take you up _____ your offer.
3. Use expressions with different verb tenses.	a. We _____ bored to death at the party, so we left early. b. I'm not going to go home yet. I _____ it out until the end. c. What did he say? My mind _____, so I don't know what he's talking about. d. You kids _____ around since you've been home. Now it's time to sit down and do your homework.

3. Error Correction

Find the errors and make corrections. One item is correct.

1. The last election sparked my interest on politics, so I'm going to study political science.

2. What drag! It's raining, so we can't have the party outside.

3. We've had awful lot of rain lately.

4. They said they bored to death at the baseball game yesterday.

5. Be careful. Your wallet is sticking it out of your pocket.

6. Their daughter fools around too much her friends and doesn't study enough.

7. Yesterday it dawned in me why you really don't want to take that job.

8. We took him up his offer and went sailing yesterday. It was great.

9. What it comes down to is that they don't pay enough attention to her.

10. They're very busy. They can take a vacation only once blue moon.

4. Choosing the Idiom

Read this review of a recent Hollywood movie. Fill in the blanks with the best possible expressions from the list. Pay special attention to how the expressions are used grammatically. You may need to consider verb tenses, subject-verb agreement, pronouns, active vs. passive voice, etc. Not all of the expressions can be used. After you finish, practice reading the sentences aloud.

I, 14

bored to death	it dawned on	once in a blue moon
fool around	stick it out	mind is wandering
an awful lot of	stick out	buckle down
be on the edge of one's seat		

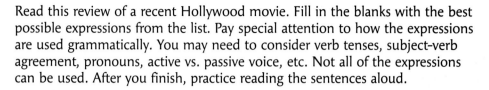

Reviews | Daily News

AT THE MOVIES

MILES ROPER

Last night I had the opportunity to see the kind of movie that comes out only (1) _____. I went in thinking that I'd be (2) _____, but I was completely surprised. It was terrific. The audience was so involved that no one was even eating popcorn. As for me, well, I was (3) _____ for most of the movie.

Why was it so interesting? I'll tell you why. It was about what (4) _____ _____ people care about—love and friendship. A woman was married to a guy who didn't work. She tried and tried to get him to (5) _____ _____ and go back to school and get a job. But no, he wouldn't. She didn't know what to do.

Then, one day she was sitting on her porch, thinking about her life. Her (6) _____ from one subject to another, when all of a sudden, (7) _____ her that she had the power to make a change in her life. She realized she didn't have to (8) _____ with this guy. Just at that moment her husband joined her on the porch and had a few of his own things to say. He asked her why she didn't work, why she (9) _____ in the house all day. Do you want to know how she responded? Well, folks, see the movie. You won't regret it.

5. Sentence Writing

Write three false sentences and one true sentence about yourself or your life for each group of expressions. Use any verb tense, and make some sentences negative. Read your sentences to your classmates. They will try to guess which sentence in each group is true. (*Variation:* Write three true sentences and one false sentence.)

Group 1	Group 2
bored to death	once in a blue moon
fool around	it dawned on me
an awful lot	my mind was wandering
be on the edge of one's seat	take someone up on

1,15

6. Dictation

You will hear the dictation three times. First, just listen. Second, as you listen, write the dictation on a piece of paper. Skip lines. Third, check what you have written.

Key Words: required, professor

7. Questions for Discussion and/or Writing

Discussion: You can answer these questions orally in groups or in the *Walk and Talk* activity in Appendix B.

Writing: You can write your own answers to these questions, or you can write the responses that you received from students during the *Walk* and *Talk* activity.

Questions

1. What are two or three things that bore you to death?

2. Think of a situation that you couldn't stand being in (perhaps a party, a wedding, a trip, or a show). Did you stick it out to the end? Why or why not?

3. Which subjects that you have studied in school sparked your interest? Which bored you to tears?

4. Were you ever a lazy student? If yes, did you eventually buckle down and become more serious about doing your work? Explain.

5. What kind of food do you like an awful lot? What kind of people do you like an awful lot? Why?

6. In what situations do you often find your mind wandering?

7. Everyone has had the experience of being on the edge of their seat at some kind of show, movie, or other type of performance. Describe one experience that you have had.

8. Role Play or Write a Monologue

In the cartoon, Steve is talking to an audience of high school students. He is telling them about his past life—how he used to be very lazy and didn't take school seriously.

Role play or write what Steve is saying. Try to use some expressions from this lesson. Refer to or write on the board the list of expressions on page 50. Also, try to use other expressions that you know. But don't feel that it is necessary to have an idiom in every sentence.

Possible starting line: *This is a picture of me when I was 16.*

9. Connection to the Real World

A. Culture and Language on the Internet

Web sites related to our lesson theme   Find information on the Internet about things to do if you're bored. Key word: *boredom.* Or, look for sites about *learning style inventories, learning styles,* and *multiple intelligences.* These sites explain the different ways people learn. If possible, have your classmates complete a learning style inventory so they can discover their own learning styles. From what is said in the introductory conversation of this lesson, speculate on Jan's and Steve's learning styles.

Informally in a group or formally in a short speech, report back to your class on some specific new information that you learned. Perhaps different students can explain the various learning styles and multiple intelligences.

> Speech Instructions—
> Appendix C

Guest Speaker—
Appendix E

If you are at a school where there is a counseling department, invite a counselor to talk to your class about learning styles and multiple intelligences. Listen, take notes, and ask the speaker questions.

Idiom Web site/General Web sites   Search an idiom web site and other sites on the Internet with the expression *on the edge of my seat* or other idioms from this lesson. Find one or two contexts in which this expression is used. Share what you found with your class.

Phrase origin Web site   Find the origin of idioms and other expressions on the Internet. Key words: *phrase origins*. Choose one expression, explain it to your classmates, and give the origin of the expression.

B. Contact Assignment

In this lesson, you learned phrasal verbs with **stick** and **take**. To learn more expressions with these words, with a partner ask a native speaker of English to help you fill out this chart. (For guidelines on how to do this kind of assignment, see Appendix F, "Contact Assignments," on page 197.)

Pronunciation Note: Remember to stress the second part of phrasal verbs.

	Meaning	Sample Sentence
stick		
up for someone	_____	_____
around	_____	_____
with	_____	_____
take		
over	_____	_____
after	_____	_____
someone up on something	_____	_____

10. Expression Collection

Every week, find three expressions from the real world that are new to you. Keep an inventory in your notebook or on index cards, following the format in Appendix G, "Expression Collection," on page 198. Be ready to share what you found in small groups or with your entire class.

On the Streets— Living from Hand to Mouth

Theme: Homelessness

Warm-Up

1. In the circles, write down whatever words come to your mind when you hear the word "homeless." Then compile everyone's list on the board.

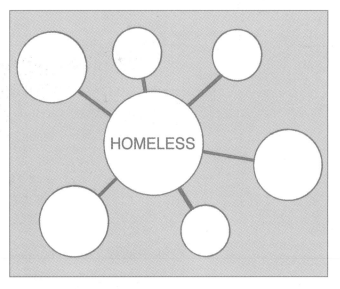

HOMELESS

2. What do you think Victor Hugo meant when he said the following in 1862?

"Do not ask the name of a person who seeks a bed for the night. He who is reluctant to give his name is the one who most needs shelter."

Focused Listening

Before You Listen

Look at the title of this lesson and look at the cartoon. What do you think the two men are saying to each other?

As You Listen

1,16

(A) **Close your book. Listen to the conversation between a homeless man and a reporter to find the answers to these questions.**

Has the homeless man always been poor?   Why was his wife unhappy?

(B) **Listen again but this time read the conversation as you listen.**

HOMELESS MAN:	Hello, young man! What brings you to **this neck of the woods**?
REPORTER:	Actually, I was wondering if I could interview you for my newspaper.
HOMELESS MAN:	Me? About what?
REPORTER:	Well, we're doing a series of articles on the homeless, and I . . .
HOMELESS MAN:	And you want to know what happened to me, what I **live on,** what it's like to **live from hand to mouth** . . .
REPORTER:	Uh, yeah. I do want to know. Would you be willing to tell me your story?
HOMELESS MAN:	You got about three hours?
REPORTER:	Whatever we need.
HOMELESS MAN:	Well then, go ahead and sit down.
REPORTER:	Thanks. Um, let's see, well, first I'd like to ask you . . .
HOMELESS MAN:	No questions. Just listen. You think I grew up poor, don't you? That I don't have an education. But you're **dead wrong.** I have a college degree. I worked for a big company. My parents **would turn over in their graves** if they could see me now.
REPORTER:	But how . . . ?
HOMELESS MAN:	I said, no questions. Just sit still and listen. In the beginning, I got up at 5:00 A.M. every day and was at work by 7:00. And I stayed at the office till 8:00 in the evening. Thirteen hours! That was the only way I could **keep up with** all the work. It just never **let up.** I never saw my family very much because when I got home, I usually went straight to bed. Well, I guess I was doing a pretty good job because I kept **moving up the ladder.** I became a manager and got more money, but I also had to work even more hours, and weekends, too. You can imagine that my wife never stopped complaining. She told me I was **getting burned out** and had no time for a life.

REPORTER:	That must've been really hard to hear.
HOMELESS MAN:	Yeah, my marriage was **at stake,** so I went to my boss and asked for a vacation. He told me to wait three more months. He needed me there. So nothing changed. **Day in and day out,** I worked and worked. Eventually my wife left. And guess what? The company **closed down** a year later! The economy was bad and I couldn't find another job. Over time, I lost everything. Hey, how many hours do you work a day?
REPORTER:	Uh, . . .
HOMELESS MAN:	Too many, I'm sure. I just hope you know what you're doing!
REPORTER:	Things could change for you, you know. You could start over. After all, you're educated.
HOMELESS MAN:	**That's wishful thinking,** young man.

After You Listen

(A) Read the sentences about the conversation. Circle *T* for *true,* *F* for *false,* or *?* if you don't know.

1.	The reporter asks the man many questions.	T F ?
2.	When the man's parents were alive, he had a job and a family.	T F ?
3.	The man worked 13 hours a day because he loved what he did.	T F ?
4.	The man still sees his children.	T F ?
5.	The man isn't optimistic about starting over.	T F ?

(B) **Guess the Meanings**
Below is a list of paraphrases of five of the idiomatic expressions in the conversation. On your own or with a partner, try to guess the five.

Paraphrase   Idiomatic Expression

1. absolutely incorrect   _____

2. went out of business   _____

3. every day   _____

4. this neighborhood   _____

5. stopped   _____

(C) **Say the conversation in pairs. Then have two students say the conversation in front of the class.**

Work with Others

If you're working with a partner or in a small group, read the short dialogues and examples for each expression aloud. Also, complete the Your Turn exercises together. Then, for each expression, circle *Yes* or *No* to show if you understand. If you circled *No,* highlight or underline what is unclear, and ask questions for clarification.

Figure It out on Your Own

Read the short dialogues and examples for each expression. Also, complete the Your Turn exercises that don't need partners. Then, for each expression, circle *Yes* or *No* to show if you understand. If you circled *No,* highlight or underline what is still unclear, and ask questions in class for clarification.

1. **in THIS (THAT) néck of the wóods** = in this area, in this place

   Note: This expression contains a touch of humor and is used in a friendly way when a person is surprised to find someone in a certain place. The word THIS receives the most stress and highest intonation to show a contrast between *THIS* place and other places.

   A: Hi Chris! What are you doing **in this neck of the woods?** I thought you moved away years ago.
   B: I did. I'm just visiting.

2. **líve on** = support oneself

   A: I have enough money to **live on** for a year without working.
   B: That's great. How did you manage that?

   A: She's **living on** unemployment insurance right now.
   B: Is it enough?

   Contrast: **live ón** = continue to live; survive
   Notice the stress on the word "on" when the expression means "continue to live."

   • It's a tragedy that he died. But he will **live ón** in our hearts.
   • Classical music has **lived ón** for centuries.

Certain things and people live on even after their time has passed. For example, John Lennon of the Beatles died at a young age, but his music lives on. What other people or things live on and on?

3. **líve from hánd to móuth** = have nothing; survive with whatever is available at the moment

   ALL CLEAR ?

   Note: This is said about people who have no income at all.

   A: How do they manage?
   B: **They live from hand to mouth.** They do some panhandling (begging) and get their meals at soup kitchens.

   Contrast: **líve from páycheck to páycheck** = make hardly enough money to last until the next check is received

   Note: This expression is used to talk about people who do work but have trouble making enough money to last from one paycheck to another.

   • They have no savings. They just **live from paycheck to paycheck,** and it's hard.

4. **be déad wróng** = be absolutely wrong

   ALL CLEAR ?

   A: If you think all the homeless are mentally ill, you'**re dead wrong.**
   B: How do you know?
   A: I've talked to a lot of homeless people, and they're totally normal.

   Other expressions with 'be dead' (meaning 'be absolutely'): **be dead tired; be dead against something**

Your Turn

Complete these sentences.

   1. Some people think that people in my native country

   _____,

   but they are dead wrong.

   2. He _____,

   so today he's dead tired.

   3. I _____

   at that restaurant. I'm dead against going there again.

5. **would turn (roll) óver in one's gráve** = would be very upset

Note: This expression refers to what a dead person would do if he or she found out about something that he or she would strongly object to. This expression is always used in a hypothetical sense, with *if* and *would.* After all, you cannot say that someone (really) turned over in his grave.

- If my grandfather saw me now (marrying someone of a different race or religion), he **would turn over in his grave.**
- If people who lived before 1900 could see the violence that's on TV and in the movies now, they **would roll over in their graves.**

Your Turn

Think of someone who has passed away (died). What is something happening today (personal, political, or social) that would make that person *turn over in his or her grave?*

6. **keep úp with something or someone** = not fall behind

- If you can't **keep up,** then maybe you're in the wrong class.
- To **keep up with** your work, you have to do your homework every night.
- The little boy with short legs had trouble **keeping up with** the tall boys who were walking fast.
- It's great that you've **kept up with** so many technological advances.

Contrast: **keep it úp** = continue

A: I got an "A" on my test, Mom!
B: Great! **Keep it up!** (or: **Keep up** the good work!)

Your Turn

Put a check (✓) next to what is hard for you to keep up with. Tell your partner why you checked those items.

_____ schoolwork	_____ housework
_____ the news	_____ gardening
_____ my e-mail	_____ changes in technology
_____ Other: _____	

7. **let úp** = gradually and finally come to a stop after a great deal of pressure (such as with work) or a great quantity of something (such as rain)

   Grammar Note: Past tense of *let* is *let;* no words can come between *let* and *up.*

   ALL CLEAR ?
   Yes No

   - If the rain **lets up,** let's go to the beach, OK?
   - The pressure finally **let up** after final exams.
   - That teacher never **lets up.** We don't have time to breathe.
   - He won't **let up.** He keeps pushing me to study.

   Contrast: **let (someone) dówn** = disappoint someone

   A: I promise that I'll get the work done.
   B: Good. Don't **let me down.** I'm relying on you.

Your Turn

Complete the chart.

Situations	Specifically, what do/did they do?
• The teacher never lets up. She makes us work very hard. • He won't let up because he wants money to buy a new computer.	She always _____ _____ _____ Every day, he _____ _____ _____ _____
• They let the children down. They were going to go to the zoo yesterday. • I let you down when you needed my help.	They _____ _____ _____ I _____ _____

8. **móve up the ládder/move úp** = advance along a career path; move up/ be promoted in a job

A: How did you **móve up the ládder** so fast?

B: I guess I worked hard and knew the right people.

Notice the stress change with the short form:

A: How did you **move úp** so fast?

B: I guess I work hard and know the right people.

1,17

Your Turn: Listening Challenge

Listen to the conversation between Joe and Ruth. Then answer the questions.

1. How does Ruth keep moving up the ladder?
2. Does she sound like a workaholic to you?
3. When she starts a family, do you think she should give up her job? Why or why not?

9. **gét burned óut** = become very tired, bored, and frustrated from doing the same work for too long (have no spark anymore, as in a fire that is going out)

- I'm **getting burned out.** I think I need to look for a different job. I've been doing this for twenty years.
- If you don't take a vacation soon, you're going to **get burned out.** You need a break.

Contrast: **be burned óut/be burnt óut** = be without any vitality or life because of overwork or working at something for too long

A: Why did he quit?

B: He **was** really **burnt (burned) out.** But now he's got a completely new career and is feeling much, much better.

Contrast: **búrnout** (noun)

Notice the stress change with the compound noun form. Stress the first part of the word.

A: Why did he quit?

B: Because of **búrnout.** But now he's much better because he's in a new job.

10. **be at stáke** = be at risk; be in danger of being lost

Spelling Note: Although they have the same pronunciation, *stake* and *steak* (meat) have entirely different meanings.

- You have to get a good lawyer to defend her. Her life is **at stake.**
- Your health is **at stake.** You have to quit smoking.
- My job is **at stake.** If I don't improve, they're going to fire me!

11. **day ín and day óut** = every day

    Note: This expression has a negative connotation. It is used to emphasize the repetitiveness of something that is done every single day.

    - I've been trying to help you **day in and day out,** but you don't listen to me.
    - She's been working on a project **day in and day out,** and if she doesn't take a break soon, I don't know what's going to happen.

12. **close dówn** = close a place permanently

    - I went downtown to the department store where I used to shop, and I was shocked to see that it was **closed down.**
    - The management threatened to **close down** the factory if there was a strike.
    - The management threatened to **close** it **down.**
    - The government plans to **close down** a lot of military bases.

13. **Thát's wíshful thínking.** = What you are saying is not likely to happen; your expression of hope is unrealistic.

    A: This lottery ticket is going to be a winner.
    B: **That's wishful thinking.**

    A: It's a holiday weekend. She won't give us homework.
    B: **That's wishful thinking.**

Your Turn

Complete the dialogue with an unrealistic statement about the future.

A: _____

B: That's wishful thinking!

NEW EXPRESSION COLLECTION

in this neck of the woods	live paycheck to paycheck	get burned out
live on	would turn over in one's grave	be at stake
be dead wrong	keep up with	day in and day out
be dead tired	keep it up	close down
be dead against	move up (the ladder)	that's wishful thinking
live from hand to mouth	let up	

1. Mini-Dialogues

Read the sentences in Column A. Choose the *best* response from Column B. Not all responses can be used. Then say each mini-dialogue with a partner.

1,18

1A	1B
___ **1.** Did you know that the minimum wage today is less than $9 an hour?	**a.** That's wishful thinking!
___ **2.** They think their kids are all going to become doctors and lawyers.	**b.** That's right. I was burned out and wanted to do something different.
___ **3.** She was arrested for selling drugs.	**c.** Her father would roll over in his grave if he knew.
___ **4.** Why do you work so much?	**d.** We're looking for an apartment. We heard the rents weren't too high around here.
___ **5.** I heard you changed jobs.	**e.** How do people live on that?
___ **6.** I heard you lost your job.	**f.** Because I plan to move up the ladder fast.
___ **7.** What are you two doing in this neck of the woods?	**g.** So many people live from hand to mouth.
	h. That's right. My company closed down, and I'm not sure what I'm going to do.

2A	2B
___ **1.** His life is at stake. He needs an operation immediately.	**a.** Don't worry about me. I know what I'm doing.
___ **2.** You're working so hard, you're going to get burned out before you're 30!	**b.** I know you won't. I can always rely on you.
___ **3.** She just won't let up. Every day she talks about moving out.	**c.** Thanks. He'll live on in our hearts.
___ **4.** Slow down! I can't keep up with you.	**d.** Sorry. I'm always in a hurry.
___ **5.** Did I really get an "A"?	**e.** You certainly did. Keep up the good work!
___ **6.** I promise I'll help you. I won't let you down.	**f.** That must really upset her parents.
___ **7.** I heard your favorite singer died. I'm so sorry.	**g.** They're dead wrong!
	h. Where do I sign to give permission?

2. Grammar Practice

Follow the directions and complete the sentences.

Directions	Sentences
1. Add an article.	a. What are you doing in this neck of _____ woods? b. If you want to move up _____ ladder, work hard!
2. Add a preposition.	a. Day _____ and day out, we study English. b. Our friendship is _____ stake. Let's talk! c. So many people live _____ paycheck _____ paycheck. d. If my grandmother knew, she'd turn over _____ her grave. e. They saved enough money to live _____ for two years without working!
3. Add a pronoun to each phrasal verb.	a. You're doing great work. Keep _____ up! b. They promised to help us move, but they didn't come. They really let _____ down. c. The owners closed down the factory two years ago. → They closed _____ down.
4. Make phrasal verbs that can't be separated.	a. After being in the same job for 30 years, he was burned _____. b. She moved _____ in the company very fast. c. When the rain lets _____, let's take a walk. d. It's hard to keep _____ _____ all this work!

3. Error Correction

Find the errors and make corrections. (*Hint:* Two sentences have correct grammar, but they have problems with meaning.) One item is correct.

1. She was burn out so she quit her job.

2. It's hard to live in one salary, so he has two jobs.

3. I eat breakfast day in and day out.

4. They closed down the store at 5:00 and they'll reopen tomorrow at 10:00.

5. My grade at stake. I need an 'A' on the next test to keep my average.

6. You can move up the ladder very quickly in this company.

7. My friend kept asking me to go to the concert and didn't let me up.

8. My boss said, "You did a great job! Keep it up the good work!"

9. I couldn't keep up that class, so I changed levels.

10. If she knew, she turns over in her grave.

4. Choosing the Idiom

Recently Julie had a terrible nightmare. Below is everything about it that she remembers. Fill in the blanks with the best possible expressions from the list. Pay special attention to how the expressions are used grammatically. You may need to consider verb tenses, subject-verb agreement, pronouns, active vs. passive voice, etc. Not all of the expressions can be used. After you finish, practice reading the sentences aloud.

let up	that's wishful thinking
at stake	live from hand to mouth
close down	get burned out
dead wrong	day in and day out
keep up with	in this neck of the woods

Oh, my nightmare was terrible! At first, I was in a big classroom with around a thousand people. The professor wrote the homework assignment on the board—read five hundred pages in two days. He also gave us three lab reports to write and announced a big test. He just wouldn't (1) _____ _____. But the other students looked happy. I was the only one who seemed worried about how to (2) _____ the work.

   Then I remember I was in the library. I was trying to read all those pages. I was reading, but I couldn't remember anything, so I started to panic. Then, all of a sudden, my professor was sitting next to me. He asked me the strangest question: "What are you doing (3) _____ _____?" I looked at him like he was crazy and told him that I was trying to do the work that he had assigned, and that I was upset because I couldn't remember anything I was reading. Then he asked me why I cared so much, and I told him that my grade was (4) _____ _____. I needed an 'A' in the class. When he heard this, he smiled and said, (5) "_____. You'll never get an 'A'!"

   Then he told me to close the book. He wanted to tell me what it was like when he was a student. (6) _____ he studied, and studied. But he never complained, and he never (7) _____. He told me that I went to too many movies and parties. I told him that he was (8) _____ _____. I was a good student, but I was tired. He then asked me what the problem was—that he had assigned only fifty pages to read.

   That's when I woke up. What a relief to realize it was just a dream! But it seemed so real. I guess it shows that I'm under a lot of pressure these days.

5. Sentence Writing

Write three false sentences and one true sentence about yourself or your life for each group of expressions. Use any verb tense, and make some sentences negative. Read your sentences to your classmates. They will try to guess which sentence in each group is true. (*Variation:* Write three true sentences and one false sentence.)

Group 1	Group 2
live on	burned out
dead against	day in and day out
keep up (with)	let someone down
move up	dead tired

6. Dictation

1,20

You will hear the dictation three times. First, just listen. Second, as you listen, write the dictation on a piece of paper. Skip lines. Third, check what you have written.

Key Words: revealed, degree, eventually

7. Questions for Discussion and/or Writing

Discussion: You can answer these questions orally in groups or in the *Walk and Talk* activity in Appendix B.

Writing: You can write your own answers to these questions, or you can write the responses that you received from students during the *Walk and Talk* activity.

Questions

1. Is there a minimum wage in your native country? Is it enough for people to live on?

2. Is it common for people you know to live from paycheck to paycheck, or do they actually save money?

3. What does a person need to do to move up the ladder in your native country? Are the opportunities to move up the same for men and women? Explain.

4. Do you know anyone who has worked too much day in and day out and then has gotten burned out? If yes, explain the situation.

5. What do you think are some steps that need to be taken to end homelessness?

8. Role Play or Write a Dialogue

In the cartoon, the reporter from the introductory conversation is now interviewing a businesswoman, Ms. Greenway. Ms. Greenway had a very difficult past—for a few years she was unemployed, and then later she had jobs that she didn't like. But now she is very successful. She talks about her past and what she did to overcome her problems and become a success.

Role play or write their conversation. Try to use some expressions from this lesson. Refer to or write on the board the list of expressions on page 66. Also, try to use other expressions that you know. But don't feel that it is necessary to have an idiom in every sentence.

Possible starting line: *I heard that years ago you had a very difficult life.*

9. Connection to the Real World

A. Culture and Language on the Internet

Web sites related to our lesson theme   Find information on the Internet about *one* of the following: homelessness; workaholics/burnout; the *glass ceiling*; nightmares. You can use these words as key words.

Informally in a group or formally in a short speech, report back to your class on some specific new information that you learned.

Speech Instructions—
Appendix C

OR

Panel Discussion—Appendix D

Take roles and conduct a panel discussion on steps to take to end homelessness. Possible roles: psychologist, homeless person, relative of homeless person, social worker, politician, teacher, police officer. Look for information on the Internet that you might use in your role on the panel.

OR

Guest Speaker—Appendix E

If you are at a school where there is a sociology department, invite a teacher or student from that department to talk to your class about the problem of homelessness. Listen, take notes, and ask the speaker questions.

Idiom Web site   In this lesson, you learned two idioms with words related to parts of the body: *this <u>neck</u> of the woods* and *from <u>hand</u> to <u>mouth</u>.* Find other idioms that have words related to parts of the body. Key words: *idioms, body.*

Proverb Web site   Search the Internet for proverbs that come from your native culture. Choose two proverbs to share with your class.

Phrase origins Web site   Find the origin of idioms and other expressions on the Internet. Key words: *phrase origins.* Choose one expression, explain it to your classmates, and give the origin of the expression.

B. Contact Assignment

In this lesson, you learned phrasal verbs with **live** and **keep**. To learn more expressions with these words, with a partner ask a native speaker of English to help you fill out this chart. (For guidelines on how to do this kind of assignment, see Appendix F, "Contact Assignments," on page 197.)

Pronunciation Note: Remember to stress the second part of phrasal verbs.

	Meaning	Sample Sentence
live		
through	_____	_____
up to	_____	_____
it up	_____	_____
keep		
off	_____	_____
at it	_____	_____

10. Expression Collection

Every week, find three expressions from the real world that are new to you. Keep an inventory in your notebook or on index cards, following the format in Appendix G, "Expression Collection," on page 198. Be ready to share what you found in small groups or with your entire class.

Collocation Match-Up

Collocations are special combinations of words. Collocations can be idioms or other phrases and expressions. Find collocations from *Lessons 3 and 4* by matching the words from Column A with the words in Column B. Sometimes more than one answer is possible. (You will probably be able to make additional expressions that are not from Lessons 3 and 4. Put these in the box.)

A

1. buckle ___down___
2. close _____
3. keep _____
4. keep it _____
5. an awful _____
6. fool _____
7. live _____
8. live from _____
9. once in a _____
10. day in and _____
11. at _____
12. what it comes _____
13. be burned _____
14. it dawned _____
15. be dead _____
16. let someone _____
17. move _____
18. on the edge _____
19. stick _____
20. take you _____

B

up

up on your invitation

up with

up the ladder

hand to mouth

tired

of my seat

around

stake

day out

down ✓

down

down

down to is that . . .

on

lot

on me that . . .

out

out

blue moon

Additional Collocations

Crossword Puzzle

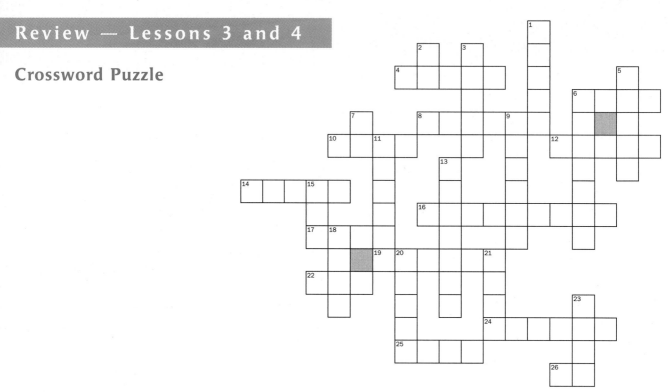

Across

4 It was awful. I was bored to ___.

6 They are so poor that they live ___ hand to mouth.

8 It's time to ___ down and get to work.

10 We go there ___ in a blue moon.

12 What it ___ down to is that we have no choice.

14 When I was unemployed. I lived from hand to ___.

16 What did you say? I'm sorry. My mind was ___.

17 The game was so exciting, we were on the ___ of our seats.

19 It just ___ on me that I should have been there.

22 ___ in and day out, we work and work.

24 If they knew, they'd turn over in their ___.

25 When the rain ___ up, let's go for a walk.

26 Thanks. I think I'll take you ___ on that.

Down

1 I'm really worried. My grade's at ___. Can you help me after class?

2 Don't let ___ down. You made a promise.

3 Don't give up. Can't you ___ it out for another few weeks?

5 You ___ up the ladder pretty fast, didn't you?

6 Come on, everyone. Stop ___ around and get to work!

7 Do you think we can live ___ $100 a month?

9 He moved up the ___ really fast, didn't he?

11 When the store ___ down, a lot of people lost jobs.

13 They're dead ___ going, so we have to go alone.

15 What were you doing in that neck of ___ woods?

18 He's ___ wrong. I didn't say that.

20 An ___ lot of people were there. It was very crowded.

21 I spent all day cleaning my house. What a ___!

23 Slow down, you guys! I can't ___ up with you.

Winning the Lottery— He's Got It Made

Theme: Luck

Warm-Up

If there is a lottery in your native country, answer the following questions and give explanations.

1. Do many people participate? Do you? Have you ever won?
2. Do winners get a lot of publicity?
3. Is any money collected from the lottery sent to the school system or used in another way for the public?

Before You Listen

Look at the title of this lesson and look at the cartoon. What do you think is going on?

As You Listen

1,21

A Close your book. Listen to the conversation to find the answers to these questions.

How does Michael feel about winning the lottery?
What is he worried about?

B Listen again, but this time read the conversation as you listen.

JENNIE:	**What's gotten into** Michael? What's he doing?
PETE:	**I haven't the slightest idea.** Look, he's coming over to us.
MICHAEL:	And these are for you.
JENNIE:	What's the occasion?
MICHAEL:	You haven't heard? I won the lottery yesterday. Ten million dollars!
JENNIE:	Ten million dollars? Come on. **That's unheard of!** Are you sure?
MICHAEL:	**Beyond the shadow of a doubt.** 6, 12, 22, 24, 25, and 28. I got every number. And it was the first time I ever bought a lottery ticket.
PETE:	Beginner's luck, I guess. How do you feel?
MICHAEL:	I'm in shock, **to say the least.** This is really all **beyond my comprehension.** It hasn't **sunk in** yet . . . maybe it never will.
JENNIE:	Well, **I've got to hand it to you.** You sure look very calm. If I were in your shoes, I don't think I'd be able to stand still, **let alone** buy presents for people and have conversations with them.
MICHAEL:	I'm not so calm. I really have no idea what's **in store** for me. You know, right now my whole life'**s up in the air.** I'm worried about **making the most of** this . . . I don't want all that money to **go down the drain.** I'm going to need some time to think.
PETE:	Are you going to quit your job?
MICHAEL:	I can't say yet. But I won't **rule it out.**
JENNIE:	Well, you're right not to make any quick decisions. And you know, you should **be on the lookout** for people who want to take advantage of you.
MICHAEL:	I know. I plan to be very, very careful.
PETE:	Well, no matter what you do, with ten million dollars, **you've got it made!**

After You Listen

(A) Read the sentences about the conversation. Circle *T* for *true*,
F for *false*, or *?* if you don't know.

1.	Michael has been playing the lottery for years.	T	F	?
2.	Jennie and Pete are jealous of Michael.	T	F	?
3.	Michael looks calm.	T	F	?
4.	Michael is calm.	T	F	?
5.	Michael might quit his job.	T	F	?

(B) **Guess the Meanings**
Below is a list of paraphrases of five of the idiomatic expressions
in the conversation. On your own or with a partner, try to guess
the five.

Paraphrase	Idiomatic Expression
1. I really don't know	_____
2. that doesn't happen	_____
3. taking total advantage of	_____
4. you're a success	_____
5. what happened to	_____

(C) Say the conversation in groups of three. Then have three students
say the conversation in front of the class.

Understanding the New Expressions

Work with Others

If you're working with a partner or in a small group, read the short
dialogues and examples for each expression aloud. Also, complete the
Your Turn exercises together. Then, for each expression, circle *Yes* or *No*
to show if you understand. If you circled *No*, highlight or underline what
is unclear, and ask questions for clarification.

Figure It out on Your Own

Read the short dialogues and examples for each expression. Also
complete the Your Turn exercises that don't need partners. Then, for
each expression, circle *Yes* or *No* to show if you understand. If you circled
No, highlight or underline what is still unclear, and ask questions in class
for clarification.

1. **Whát's gótten ínto (someone)?** What has happened to (someone)?

   Note: This is a question you might ask when you see that someone you know is acting in an unusual way.

   Pronunciation Note: Give the highest intonation to the word *into:*

   What's gotten ᶦⁿᵗᵒ you?

   A: You haven't smiled all day. **What's gotten into** you?
   B: Nothing. I'm tired, that's all.

   A: I've never seen her so happy. **What's gotten into** her?
   B: I wonder. Let's go ask.

Your Turn

Think of a friend or relative whose behavior seemed to suddenly change (becoming very happy or angry). Did you say something to anyone equivalent to the expression "What's gotten into him/her?" Explain the circumstances.

2. **nót háve (gót) the slíghtest ídea = háve nó idéa = nót háve a clúe*** = not know at all

   Note: It is not possible to put this expression in the affirmative. You cannot say *I have the slightest idea.*

   A: Do you know what time it is?
   B: { **I haven't (got) the slightest idea.**
       I have no idea.
       I don't have a clue.
   I never wear my watch when I'm on vacation.

   A: Do you think he knows about the surprise party?
   B: I'm sure he { **doesn't have the slightest idea.**
                  has no idea.
                  doesn't have a clue.
   We kept all the plans a secret.

   Two other ways to emphasize that you don't know something: **"Béats mé!"** and **"Yóur gúess is as góod as míne!"** (These expressions are quite informal; you would use them only with close friends or family members.)

   A: Do you know what time it is?
   B: **Beats me!**

   A: I wonder where they left the key.
   B: **Your guess is as good as mine.**

   *For more information on "not have a clue," see Lesson 2.

3. Thát's unhéard of = That's unbelievable; that never happens.

Note: This is said when something is so unusual that it is not "heard of."

ALL CLEAR ?Yes No

A: In some countries, students go to school on Saturdays.
B: **That's unheard of** here.

A: They're paid only $2 an hour.
B: **That's unheard of** here. How can they live on that?

4. beyond the shádow of a dóubt = absolutely sure/certain, with no doubt at all

Note: Some people say "beyond *a* shadow of a doubt."

ALL CLEAR ?Yes No

A: Are you sure? Is she really pregnant?
B: Yes. **Beyond the shadow of a doubt.**

• In the U.S. legal system, a person is considered innocent until proven guilty **beyond the shadow of a doubt.**

Your Turn: Listening Challenge

Listen to the conversation between the police officer and Mr. Walker. Then answer the questions.

1. What is Mr. Walker sure about beyond the shadow of a doubt?
2. Does his wife have a good alibi?
3. What crime do you think his wife is being accused of?

ALL CLEAR ?
Yes   No

5. **to sáy the léast** = to say the minimum

Note: This is said when it is possible to use a stronger adjective or description, but you couldn't.

A: I work eight hours a day, go to school three hours a day, and have two young children. I'm tired [~~I'm stressed, impatient, and exhausted~~], **to say the least.**

B: You should be tired. I don't know how you do it!

• We have great jobs and a nice place to live. We're very lucky, **to say the least.**

ALL CLEAR ?
Yes   No

6. **beyond one's comprehénsion (that)** = very hard to believe; outside one's ability to understand (*beyond* means far away)

Note: This is said when it is very hard or impossible to believe/understand something.

• I find calculus **beyond my comprehension.** Probably it's because I never learned algebra well.

• It's **beyond my comprehension that** so many people can live in such a small area.

• Nobody can believe that she committed the crime. It's **beyond our comprehension that** she could break the law.

Your Turn

Think about something strange in the world and complete this sentence.

It's beyond my comprehension that _____

_____

7. **sink ín** = be gradually believed or understood

Grammar Note: This verb cannot be separated.

Grammar Note: When something sinks in the water, it typically goes down slowly. When information that is difficult to understand or believe enters the brain, it "sinks in" slowly until it is clearly understood.

• When they heard the news that the war was over, they didn't believe it at first. It took time for the news to **sink in.**

A: You're married? But you're only 18!
B: Uh-huh. We got married last week.
A: I've got to sit down and let this **sink in.** I don't believe it.

A: Maybe after I study this for six hours or so, it'll all **sink in.**
B: I hope so. The test is tomorrow.

Your Turn

Tell a partner about some news that you once heard that took time to sink in. (This would be news that was a good or bad shock, that was hard to believe at first.)

8. **I've gót to hánd it to you.** = I have to give (you) credit for something because you did a good job.

Pronunciation Note: Give the highest intonation to the word, "hand:"
I've got to ^hand it to you.

• **I've got to hand it to you.** You managed to get all your work done on time, and I know you were sick.
• **I've got to hand it to you.** You won all that money in the lottery, but you didn't change. You're still the great person you always were.

9. **lét alóne** = It is certainly impossible to . . . /Someone certainly can't/won't . . .

Note: This is said as a strong negative response to a question or suggestion. Here is the typical conversational pattern with this expression:

Question: Why don't you X?
Answer: We can't Y (Y is easier to do than X), **let alone** X.

A: Why don't you fly to Mexico?
B: We can't afford to drive, **let alone** fly.

Easier thing to do		*Harder thing to do*
I can't walk fast,	→	**let alone** run.
It's difficult to speak English,	→	**let alone** write essays.
I can't speak English,	→	**let alone** understand the culture.
I don't want to take a walk,	→	**let alone** climb that mountain.

Contrast: **léave (someone or something) alóne** = stay away from

- Please **leave me alone.** I don't feel like talking right now. (This might be said to someone you know very well.)
- **Leave** my papers **alone.** I don't want anyone to touch them. (Because this is a command, it is not very polite.)

Your Turn

Complete these three sentences with verbs that show things that are difficult for you to do.

a. I can't _____, let alone _____.

b. It's difficult to _____, let alone _____.

c. I don't want to _____, let alone _____.

10. **be in stóre (for someone)** = be waiting to happen in the future

A: There's a surprise **in store for** you when you get home.
B: What is it?
A: I'm not going to tell you. You just have to wait!

A: There are going to be some big changes around here soon.
B: Do you know what's **in store** for me?
A: I'm afraid you might lose your job.

MOM: You know what's **in store** when you misbehave, don't you?

CHILD: I know.

MOM: Now play quietly or you'll have to go to your room.

11. be úp in the aír = be undecided

ALL CLEAR ?

A: Are you going to take the new job and move?
B: We're not sure. Everything's **up in the air.** There's a chance we might stay here if I can get a higher salary.

A: When's the wedding?
B: I don't know. Now they're saying they're not going to get married, that they're just going to live together. It's all **up in the air.**
A: Their parents must love that. (This is a sarcastic remark: the speaker means exactly the opposite of what he or she is saying.)

12. máke the móst of (something) = get the most from something; take advantage of something

ALL CLEAR ?

A: We have one more day here, and we're going to **make the most of** it. We're going to eat at the best restaurant and walk around all night.
B: Aren't you going to sleep?
A: No way. We want to take advantage of every second. Who knows? We may never come back!

A: Do you think this is the wrong day for the party?
B: It must be—there's no one here. But since we've driven so far, let's **make the most of** it and look around town before we go back home.

13. gó dówn the dráin = be wasted

Note: When something *goes down the drain,* it is lost.

- The electricity went out, and I didn't save my work on the computer. All those hours of work **went down the drain.**
- They won a few hundred dollars at the casino, but it all **went down the drain** because they lost it the next day.

Your Turn

Complete the dialogue with sentences about when you worked hard on something that failed, or when you lost a lot of time or money. Use the expression *go down the drain.*

A: What's wrong?

B: _____

14. rule (something or someone) óut = say that something is impossible or that it can't happen

Origin Note: This expression probably comes from drawing a line through written material with a ruler.

A: Dad, can't we go to Disneyland®?

B: Maybe. I won't **rule it out,** but there are other places we're thinking of for vacation.

- It's too dangerous to travel there, so we have to **rule it out.**
- The doctor won't **rule out** a broken bone until he's seen an X-ray.
- The police arrested someone yesterday, but then they **ruled her out** because the witness didn't identify her.

15. **be on the lóokout (for)** = be constantly looking carefully for someone
or something

ALL CLEAR ?

- Airport officials **are** always **on the lookout** for any suspicious packages
  or people.
- We'**re on the lookout** for people who can do some good translations.
  Will you let us know if you know anyone?
- It's important to **be on the lookout for** fires during the summer.

16. **have gót it máde/háve it máde** = be sure of success

ALL CLEAR ?

A: He'**s got it made.** (or: He **has it made.**) He has a great job, a great
girlfriend, and . . .
B: Are you jealous?

A: You think all those famous stars **have (got) it made** don't you? Well,
you know, not all of them are so happy. Look at the number of divorces.
B: You may have a point.

- If you've got a good education and speak a few languages, **you've got it
  made.** You'll have no trouble finding a job.

NEW EXPRESSION COLLECTION

What's gotten into	to say the least	up in the air
I haven't the slightest idea	beyond my comprehension	make the most of
beats me	sink in	go down the drain
your guess is as good as mine	I've got to hand it to you	rule out
that's unheard of	let alone	be on the lookout
beyond the shadow of a doubt	in store	have (got) it made

Exercises

(See page 162 for pronunciation exercises for Lesson 5.)

1,23

1. Mini-Dialogues

Read the sentences in Column A. Choose the *best* response from Column B. Not all responses can be used. Then say each mini-dialogue with a partner.

1A	1B
d __ **1.** I don't believe it! Are you sure?	**a.** The electricity went out and I didn't save my work on the computer. All my work went down the drain.
a __ **2.** You look really upset. What happened?	**b.** To say the least, I think it's a great idea.
e __ **3.** I'm on the lookout for a good used car.	**c.** Take it easy. We'll still have a good time. It's a great meal, so let's make the most of it.
c __ **4.** They called and canceled dinner tonight. After we did all that cooking!	**d.** Uh-huh. Beyond the shadow of a doubt.
f __ **5.** When's our next test?	**e.** I'll keep my eyes open. If I see one, I'll call you.
	f. Beats me!

2A	2B
b __ **1.** The teacher wants us to read a whole book over the weekend.	**a.** Well, they've ruled out anything really serious, but they still have some more tests to do.
f __ **2.** That was incredible news, wasn't it?	**b.** Really? That's unheard of!
a __ **3.** What's wrong with him?	**c.** I'm doing OK.
d __ **4.** Are they going to move?	**d.** Not yet. Everything's up in the air till they hear about that job.
c __ **5.** Nice car. Looks like you've really got it made.	**e.** Just try to make the most of it.
	f. I know. It hasn't sunk in yet. I may never believe it.

3A	3B
a f __ **1.** It's so hot, it's hard to think, let alone work.	**a.** Why don't we take a break?
e __ **2.** Wait till you hear what we have in store for you!	**b.** Thanks, I tried, and it wasn't easy, believe me.
b __ **3.** I've got to hand it to you. You dealt with that situation very well.	**c.** Neither do I.
d f __ **4.** It's absolutely beyond my comprehension that they could do that.	**d.** I know what you mean. I don't know what got into them.
c __ **5.** I don't have the slightest idea about what happened last night.	**e.** It sure sounds like it's going to be something special.
	f. She wants everyone to leave her alone.

2. Grammar Practice

Follow the directions and complete the sentences.

Directions	Sentences
1. Add an article.	a. I'm sorry, but I don't have _____ clue. b. I'm sorry, but I don't have _____ slightest idea. c. This grammar is confusing, to say _____ least. d. Back up your work, or it can all go down _____ drain.
2. Add a preposition.	a. What's gotten _____ them? b. That can't be true! That's unheard _____! c. She broke the mirror, and I know what's _____ store _____ her!
3. Add articles and prepositions.	a. When you're in a crowd, be _____ lookout _____ pickpockets. b. Try to make _____ most _____ your opportunities. c. Their plans are still up _____ air. d. I'm sure, beyond _____ shadow _____ doubt.
4. Add a form of *got*.	a. They're very successful. They've _____ it made. b. I haven't _____ the slightest idea. c. What's _____ into them? d. I've _____ to hand it to you. You did a great job!

3. Error Correction

Find the errors and make corrections. One item is correct.

1. A: What time is the party?

   B: I don't know. Your guess is good as mine!

2. A: Can you believe it? He's 40 and he's been married six times.

   B: Unheard of!

3. A: They're going to have quintuplets? What are they going to do?

   B: I have no idea. They have trouble supporting themselves, leave alone five children.

4. A: Does he have a chance of getting the job?

   B: I don't know. He's going to have an interview, so they haven't ruled out him.

5. Can you give me a minute to let this news sink in?

6. A: Are you sure? Everyone is going to get a 10% raise?

   B: Uh-huh. Beyond shadow of a doubt.

7. She's been laughing and singing all day. What gotten into her?

8. I got to hand it to you. You did a great job!

9. Idioms are hard to learn, to say least!

10. I haven't got slightest idea where I am. I'm totally lost!

4. Choosing the Idiom

The following is an e-mail that Michael, the lottery winner, has received from his mother. She lives in another city in a small apartment. She is a widow, and has never had much money. For most of her adult life she worked very hard to make sure her son had a good education, so that he could get a good job.

Fill in the blanks with the best possible expressions from the list. Pay special attention to how the expressions are used grammatically. You may need to consider verb tenses, subject-verb agreement, pronouns, active vs. passive voice, etc. Not all of the expressions can be used. After you finish, practice reading the sentences aloud.

to say the least   go down the drain   beyond ____ comprehension
sink in   be on the lookout   be in store
let alone   not have the slightest idea   make the most of
be up in the air   beyond the shadow of a doubt   have it made

---

From: "Dorothy Wynn" <dorwynn@postmail.com>
To: <michaelwynn@netster.net>
Subject: some maternal advice
Date: Mon, 10 Jan

Hi Michael,

I still don't believe your news. I don't know if it will ever (1) _____ _____. I saw you on TV tonight and am very happy for you, (2) _____ _____. You looked so happy and healthy! That's all a mother can want.

The phone hasn't stopped ringing. Everyone is sending their congratulations. At this point, I can hardly think, (3) _____ write, but I'm going to try to write because a lot of thoughts are jumping around in my mind and I need to get them down.

I have to admit, I'm worried about you. Right now, you think that you (4) _____ _____, but where will you be a year from now? You have to be extremely careful. You need to constantly (5) _____, or all that money can (6) _____.

I want you to (7) _____ this time in your life. Pay all your bills, and take a trip. Enjoy yourself. I don't want anything. Find yourself a nice woman to marry, but make sure that she isn't after your money. Please promise me that you won't get married until you are convinced (8) _____ that the woman isn't a fortune hunter.

You said that your plans (9) _____. But please let me know what you decide to do. And find out how much you will have to pay in taxes. I'm sure you'll be shocked. And don't forget to give a nice amount of money to charity. You should share your wealth.

Well, I guess we can't really know exactly what (10) _____ _____, can we? I just wish you well. Don't let all this money change you, Michael.

Lots of love,
Mom

5. Sentence Writing

Write three false sentences and one true sentence about yourself or your life for the group of expressions. Use any verb tense, and make some sentences negative. Read your sentences to your classmates. They will try to guess which sentence is true. (*Variation:* Write three true sentences and one false sentence.)

> beyond my comprehension that
> let alone
> be on the lookout for
> make the most of

1,25

6. Dictation

You will hear the dictation three times. First, just listen. Second, as you listen, write the dictation on a piece of paper. Skip lines. Third, check what you have written.

Key Words: comprehension, sunk, advised, advantage

7. Questions for Discussion and/or Writing

Discussion: You can answer these questions orally in groups or in the *Walk and Talk* activity in Appendix B.

Writing: You can write your own answers to these questions, or you can write the responses that you received from students during the *Walk and Talk* activity.

Questions

1. Do you have an expression similar to "beginner's luck" in your native language? If yes, what is it? What are some symbols of good luck and bad luck in your native culture?

2. If you won millions of dollars in a lottery, what would you do with the money?

3. What is Michael's mother (in Exercise 4) worried about? Read her e-mail again, and make a list of her concerns about his sudden wealth. Add any concerns that you might have.

4. What are some American customs that are unheard of in your native country? What are some customs in your native country that are unheard of in the United States?

5. What aspects of your life are up in the air?

6. Describe a time when your efforts to do something went down the drain.

7. Describe the life of someone (real or imaginary) who's got it made.

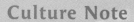

Culture Note

Many people think a rabbit's foot is a lucky charm. They believe that if you rub it, you will have good luck.

8. Role Play or Write a Dialogue

In the cartoon, a couple is "panning for gold" in gold country in California, and suddenly one of them finds a piece of gold, called a nugget. This is a very big nugget, and the woman is very excited because this may mean that they will become very wealthy. Her husband isn't so sure and he asks a lot of questions.

Role play or write their conversation. Try to use some expressions from this lesson. Refer to or write on the board the list of expressions on page 85. Also, try to use other expressions that you know. But don't feel that it is necessary to have an idiom in every sentence.

Possible starting line: *Look! There's gold in here. We're rich!!!*

9. Connection to the Real World

A. Culture and Language on the Internet

Web sites related to our lesson theme   Find information on the Internet about one or more of the following:

- superstitions. Key words: *superstitions/luck*
- urban legends. Key word: *urban legends/luck*
- the history of lotteries. Key words: *lottery (lotteries)/history*
- lotteries and education. Key words: *lottery (lotteries)/education*

Speech Instructions—
Appendix C

Informally in a group or formally in a short speech, report back to your class on some specific new information that you learned. Perhaps different students can explain various superstitions and urban legends related to luck. Other students can report on lotteries.

Idiom Web site Find translations of idioms on the Internet. Choose one expression and explain it to your classmates.

Key Words: idioms/translations

You can also search the Internet for a song using the literal interpretation of *go down the drain.* Search for Mr. Rogers, the man who hosted the children's TV show, *Mr. Rogers' Neighborhood.* Find out what he said about "going down the drain."

Key words: Mr. Rogers/drain

B. Contact Assignment

In this lesson, you learned phrasal verbs with **rule** and **sink**. To learn more expressions with these words, with a partner ask a native speaker of English to help you fill out this chart. (For guidelines on how to do this kind of assignment, see Appendix F, "Contact Assignments," on page 197.)

Pronunciation Note: Remember to stress the second part of phrasal verbs.

	Meaning	Sample Sentence
rule		
against	_____	_____ (legal meaning)
on	_____	_____ (legal meaning)
over	_____	_____ (political meaning)
sink		
one's teeth into something	_____	_____
(back) into a chair	_____	_____

10. Expression Collection

Every week, find three expressions from the real world that are new to you. Keep an inventory in your notebook or on index cards, following the format in Appendix G, "Expression Collection," on page 198. Be ready to share what you found in small groups or with your entire class.

Stuck in an Elevator— Cooped Up and Sitting Tight

Theme: Phobias

Warm-Up

1. "Phobias" are strong fears. "Claustrophobia" is the fear of being in a small space, such as in an elevator. Do you or anyone you know have any phobias?

2. Have you ever been "stuck" in any of these places? If yes, explain the situation.

- stuck in an elevator
- stuck in traffic
- stuck at an airport
- Other: _____

Focused Listening

Before You Listen

Look at the cartoon. How do you think the two people are dealing with the situation? What do you think they are saying?

As You Listen

(A) Close your book. Listen to the conversation between Mrs. Calm and Mr. Claustrophobia* to find the answers to these questions.

How is Mrs. Calm handling the situation?
How does she try to get Mr. Claustrophobia to calm down?

2,1

Ⓑ Listen again, but this time read the conversation as you listen.

MR. CLAUSTROPHOBIA:	Oh, no! This can't be happening.
MRS. CALM:	Hmm. Well, that certainly happened **out of the blue.** I wonder what's going on.
MR. CLAUSTROPHOBIA:	I'm going to ring the alarm. **This is the last straw.** I told them weeks ago to check this elevator. I would have **been better off** taking the stairs.
MRS. CALM:	Do you mean this has happened before?
MR. CLAUSTROPHOBIA:	It sure has. It was a few weeks ago, but I wasn't in the elevator . . . Oh, if I**'m cooped up in** here really long, I don't know what I'm going to do. I**'m** already **at the end of my rope.**
MRS. CALM:	Well, **for crying out loud,** young man, don't **lose your head.** Just calm down, and I'm sure they'll get this thing started again as soon as they can.
MR. CLAUSTROPHOBIA:	You know, I **knocked myself out** to be on time for my meeting, and now look.
MRS. CALM:	Complaining isn't going to help. We'll just have to **make do** here, and be thankful that we have some light and some company.
MR. CLAUSTROPHOBIA:	Actually, you're right. I'm glad I'm not alone in here, or I'd be **climbing the walls.**
MRS. CALM:	So, you see—it could be a lot worse. Just please do me a favor and **keep a level head.** Let's just **sit tight** and wait for help.
MR. CLAUSTROPHOBIA:	How can you be so calm? It sounds like you've been stuck in elevators before!
MRS. CALM:	Well, the truth is, this is my first time. But why should I panic? What good would it do? I don't want to **dwell on** things that scare me. I'd rather pass the time in here pleasantly.
MR. CLAUSTROPHOBIA:	How would that ever be possible?
MRS. CALM:	Hmm, we could tell each other our life stories. Who knows, we might even **come through** this as friends!
MR. CLAUSTROPHOBIA:	Huh?
MRS. CALM:	We can help each other by doing something that'll distract us. Why don't you just sit down and tell me about yourself?

Claustrophobia is the fear of being enclosed in small spaces.

After You Listen

(A) Below are details about the introductory conversation. Circle *T* for *true*, *F* for *false*, or *?* if you don't know.

1. The elevator has gotten stuck before.   Ⓣ F ?
2. Mr. Claustrophobia will be late for his meeting.   Ⓣ F ?
3. Mrs. Calm has been stuck in an elevator before.   T Ⓕ ?
4. The two of them become friends in the elevator.   T F Ⓟ
5. Mrs. Calm is a psychologist.   T Ⓕ ?

(B) **Guess the Meanings**
Below is a list of paraphrases of five of the idiomatic expressions in the conversation. On your own or with a partner, try to guess the five.

Paraphrase	Idiomatic Expression
1. go crazy	climbing the walls
2. with no warning	out of the blue
3. be patient	sit tight
4. stuck in	cooped up in
5. think too much about	dwell on

(C) Say the conversation in pairs. Then have two students say the conversation in front of the class.

Understanding the New Expressions

Work with Others

If you're working with a partner or in a small group, read the short dialogues and examples for each expression aloud. Also, complete the Your Turn exercises together. Then, for each expression, circle *Yes* or *No* to show if you understand. If you circled *No*, highlight or underline what is unclear, and ask questions for clarification.

Figure It out on Your Own

Read the short dialogues and examples for each expression. Also, complete the Your Turn exercises that don't need a partner. Then, for each expression, circle *Yes* or *No* to show if you understand. If you circled *No*, highlight or underline what is still unclear, and ask questions in class for clarification.

ALL CLEAR ?

1. **óut of the blúe = óut of nówhere** = suddenly, from nowhere, without any warning

   Pronunciation Note: You will hear native speakers of English pronounce "out of" as "ouda"—"ouda the blue," "ouda nowhere", etc.

   A: **Out of the blue,** she told him that she was leaving. (Or: She told him she was leaving **out of the blue.**)

   B: I bet he was shocked.

   • She was speeding, but there was no one else on the road. Then, **out of the blue,** a police car came out of the trees and went after her with its sirens blaring.

   Other Expression with "out of"
   óut of the córner of one's éye = see something indirectly

   • When he was getting money from the ATM, he saw a strange person **out of the corner of his eye,** so he got scared.

ALL CLEAR ?

2. **[This/That is/was] the lást stráw** = the last one of a series of frustrating things that have happened

   Note: This last event makes a person lose all patience.

   Origin: This is a shortened version of the expression *the straw that broke the camel's back.* The origin of this expression, according to the *Morris Dictionary of Word and Phrase Origins,* is from the writing of Charles Dickens: " '. . . the last straw breaks the laden camel's back,' meaning that there is a limit to everyone's endurance, or everyone has his breaking point. Dickens was writing in the nineteenth century and he may have received his inspiration from an earlier proverb, 'Tis the last feather that breaks the horse's back.' "

- They've been late every time we've invited them to the movies, and now we're going to miss the beginning. **This is the last straw.** I'm never inviting them again.
- Do you hear those drums upstairs? I've asked them over and over again to practice before 10:00, and now it's 11:00. **This is the last straw.** I'm going to call the police.

Your Turn: Listening Challenge

Listen to the three stories. For each, find out what was *the last straw* and what action was taken.

2,2

The last straw	Action taken
1. The roommate took her book.	She moved.
2. _____	_____
3. _____	_____

3. **be bétter off** = be in a better state or condition ≠ **be wórse off**

ALL CLEAR ?

Yes   No

- Most people **are better off** today because the economy is better.
- We're the first generation to **be worse off** financially than our parents.

Grammar Note: These expressions are often followed by gerunds.

- Many people think they would have **been better off** study**ing** English when they were children. But it's never too late.

A: Wouldn't you **be better off** fly**ing** rather than driving?
B: But I want to see the sights on the way. I'm in no hurry.

Pronunciation Note: Use more stress and higher intonation on the word *off* when it comes at the end of a sentence.

- I hope the next generation will **be better óff.**

Your Turn

Ask your partner, "Are you better or worse off now than you were four years ago?" Ask for an explanation, and then form a group of four with another pair of students. Tell them what your partner said.

4. **be cooped úp (in)** = be inside a place feeling like you don't have the freedom to go out

Origin: This probably comes from the idea of a chicken coop, which is the enclosed area where chickens live.

A: How was your vacation in the mountains?

B: Not so great. There was a big storm, so we **were cooped up in** the cabin for most of the week.

• I need to get out of the house. I've **been cooped up** here for three days with a cold, and I need some fresh air.

Your Turn

Have you ever been cooped up in a car, train, bus, plane, or boat for a long trip? If yes, describe how you (and the others) felt and what you did to pass the time.

5. **be at the énd of one's rópe** = be under a lot of stress, at the breaking point

Note: If you are **at the end of your rope,** you are at a point that is not very strong and is not balanced.

A: **I'm at the end of my rope.** I can't take it anymore. There's too much pressure.

B: Don't you think you need to see a doctor? It sounds like you need some help.

A: What happened to her? I saw her run out of the office.

B: She said she **was at the end of her rope,** and she quit.

A: What was bothering her?

B: She said that nothing ever changed around here except that she kept getting more and more work that she couldn't handle. She told us that she was going to take a long vacation, and then look for a new career.

6. **For crýing out lóud!** - This is an exclamation of anger.

Note: It is best not to say this, but it is useful to understand it.

Origin: This is probably a euphemism for the exclamation "For Christ's sake!" People did not want to say that, and somehow *for crying* . . . came out as a substitute. (A euphemism is a special expression that is used to avoid saying something else. An example would be the expression *pass away,* which is often used instead of the word *die.*)

- **For crying out loud!** How many times do I have to ask you to turn out the lights?
- **For crying out loud!** Will you guys be quiet for a minute?

Another Expression with "cry:"
It's nó úse crýing over spílt mílk (or Dón't crý over spílt mílk!) = It's no use *complaining* about what is past; it cannot be changed.

A: Oh no, why did I sell my guitar?

B: I don't know. Can you get it back?

A: No.

B: Well, **it's no use crying over spilt milk. (or Don't cry over spilt milk.)** Save your money for a new one.

ALL CLEAR ?
Yes   No

7. lóse one's héad = go crazy or do a crazy thing; (sometimes) panic

A: You bought that old car???

B: Uh-huh. I don't know why I did it. I guess I **lost my head.** At the time, it looked like a good deal.

A: What did they do during the earthquake?

B: Well, some people **lost their heads** and screamed and ran outside. But others went under doorways and tables and waited for the shaking to stop.

ALL CLEAR ?
Yes   No

8. knock oneself óut = try very hard, making oneself very tired

Grammar Note: This expression can be followed by an infinitive or a gerund.

- We **knocked ourselves out** to be here even though there's a big storm, but no one else is here.
- We **knocked ourselves out** driving in the storm, but no one else is here.

Contrast: **be knocked óut** = *be very tired*

- I'm too **knocked out** to go to the movies tonight. Sorry.
- He **was** so **knocked out** that he went straight to bed.

Contrast: **knock someone óut** = hit someone on the head and cause him or her to become unconscious. This is the literal meaning of the **expression**. It is used in boxing and in fights in general.

• That fighter is going to **knock** the other guy **out** right away.

9. **máke dó** = manage with what one has, even though it isn't enough or perfect

A: How are they these days?
B: They're managing to **make do** on the little money they have. They're still looking for better jobs.

• This elevator isn't exactly comfortable, but we have no choice but to **make do.**
• During the snowstorm, we didn't have much food. But we **made do** with what we had until we could get to the store.

10. **clímb the wálls** = go crazy because of being bored, especially in an enclosed space such as a house

• I'd be **climbing the walls** if I lived in an apartment this small.
• I wonder if the rain will ever stop. The kids are **climbing the walls.**

Related Expression: **gét/háve cábin féver** = be in an enclosed space for a long time so you feel that you need to get out

• We've been cooped up so long because of the snow, I'm **getting cabin fever.**
• The kids **have cabin fever.** Let's take them out so they can run around for a while.

Your Turn

Ask three classmates one of the following questions and complete the chart.

- Tell me about one time when you were so bored that you were climbing the walls.

OR

- Tell me about one time when you or someone you know had cabin fever.

Classmate	Situation
1. _____	_____
2. _____	_____
3. _____	_____

ALL CLEAR ?

11. kéep a lével héad = keep calm

A: The fire was scary, but everyone **kept a level head** and no one panicked.

B: That's lucky. It could've been a lot worse.

Your Turn

If you were in a scary situation, who would you want to have with you? In other words, who do you know would keep a level head? Tell your partner who this person would be and why you would choose to be with him or her.

12. sít tíght (and) = stay in one place calmly and wait for something or someone

Pronunciation Note: When the sound at the end of one word is the same as the first sound of the next word, such as with siT Tight, pronounce that sound only once ("si-tight").

- **Sit tight.** Help is on the way.
- **Sit tight** and I'll be right there. Don't go anywhere.
- We need to **sit tight** and wait.

ALL CLEAR ?
Yes No

13. dwéll on = think too much about something

- Let's not **dwell on** the dangerous things that can happen while we're stuck in this elevator. Let's talk about something else.
- It's not good to **dwell on** the past so much. Think about the future.

ALL CLEAR ?
Yes No

14. come thróugh = survive a difficult situation

- I have good news for you. He **came through** the surgery beautifully. He'll be fine.
- They're lucky. Their town **came through** the war with little damage.
- They **came through** that time on the elevator as friends. In fact, they went out to a very special dinner after they were rescued.

ALL CLEAR ?
Yes No

NEW EXPRESSION COLLECTION

out of the blue	at the end of my rope	climb the walls
out of nowhere	for crying out loud	have cabin fever
out of the corner of one's eye	don't cry over spilt milk	keep a level head
this is the last straw	lose your head	sit tight
better off	knock myself out	dwell on
cooped up in	make do	come through

1. Mini-Dialogues

Read the sentences in Column A. Choose the *best* response from Column B. Not all responses can be used. Then say each mini-dialogue with a partner.

1A	1B
___ **1.** I'm at the end of my rope. I've been cooped up in the house for too long.	**a.** I don't know where to begin!
___ **2.** Chris and Debra are coming over for dinner. Do we have enough food?	**b.** Well, it looks like you came through it all right.
___ **3.** Sit tight. Don't go anywhere. I'll be right back, OK?	**c.** Please hurry. I don't want to be alone.
___ **4.** Don't dwell on the trouble you had. Tell me about the good parts of your trip.	**d.** I'm not going shopping again, so we'll have to make do with what we have.
___ **5.** The plane trip was really bumpy. There was a lot of turbulence.	**e.** I saw them out of the corner of my eye.
___ **6.** Do you think people are better off or worse off than they used to be?	**f.** You're not so sick anymore. Why don't you take a walk?
	g. It's hard to say.

2A	2B
___ **1.** For crying out loud! Where have you been?	**a.** Thanks. Maybe I'll take a few minutes.
___ **2.** This is the last straw. It's happened too many times before.	**b.** Don't cry over spilt milk!
___ **3.** Don't you think we'd be better off living on an island?	**c.** Stuck in traffic and I forgot my phone. Sorry I'm so late.
___ **4.** I'm totally shocked. Out of the blue, they said they were leaving the country forever.	**d.** Well, it depends on which one.
___ **5.** Come on. Take a break. You've been knocking yourself out for hours.	**e.** Sweet dreams!
___ **6.** I'm knocked out. I'm going to bed.	**f.** Did they say why?
	g. I know. It's my fault. I promise I won't do it again.

2. Grammar Practice

Follow the directions and complete the sentences.

	Directions	Sentences
1.	Add an article.	a. _____ last straw was when the car broke down again. b. Calm down and keep _____ level head. c. I need to go out. I'm climbing _____ walls.
2.	Add a preposition.	a. I need to go out. I've been cooped up _____ here for too long. b. _____ crying out loud! Please listen to me! c. Let's dwell _____ the good things, OK? d. We'll come _____ this difficult time. Don't worry.
3.	Add articles and prepositions.	a. She could see him out _____ corner _____ her eye. b. I hadn't heard from him in ten years, and then I got a call out _____ _____ blue. c. Be careful. The boss is really angry. He's _____ end _____ his rope.
4.	Add a gerund.	a. She knocked herself out all day _____ the house. b. They were better off _____ in their old apartment. c. Be thankful about where you live now. You'd be worse off _____ in that old house.

3. Error Correction

Find the errors and make corrections. One item is correct.

1. The speeding car came out nowhere.

2. Out the corner of my eye, I saw the child sneak a piece of candy.

3. This is last straw. I'm not going to go there anymore.

4. You'd be better off to take three classes instead of four.

5. I was coop up the library all weekend because I have three tests this week.

6. We had a difficult time, but we coming through it OK.

7. It's no use to cry over spilt milk! You can't change it.

8. They had to made do with very little money when they first arrived in this country, but now they're doing fine.

9. Sit tight to wait until they get here.

10. He's at the end of his rope. He's going to look for a new place to live.

4. Choosing the Idiom

The following conversation is between a rescue worker and the two people who are stuck in the elevator. Fill in the blanks with the best possible expressions from the list. Pay special attention to how the expressions are used grammatically. You may need to consider verb tenses, subject-verb agreement, pronouns, active vs. passive voice, etc. Not all of the expressions can be used. After you finish, practice reading the sentences aloud.

sit tight
cooped up
knock oneself out
keep a level head
dwell on
be at the end of one's rope
come through
climb the walls

RESCUE WORKER: Hello in there! How're you doing?

MR. CLAUSTROPHOBIA: Could be better! Hey, I'm sure glad to see you.

MRS. CALM: So am I. What's your name?

RESCUE WORKER: I'm Bill. And the good news is that about ten people are working hard to locate the problem and get you out of this elevator.

MR. CLAUSTROPHOBIA: You mean we can't get out yet? I can't stand being (1) _____ in here. I'm starting to (2) _____.

RESCUE WORKER: I know. Just (3) _____ and be patient for another few minutes, and I'm sure we'll be able to get this thing moving again.

MR. CLAUSTROPHOBIA: But I am (4) _____. You've got to get me out of here!

MRS. CALM: Now, Mr. Claustrophobia, you'll be just fine. Try to relax. Bill will help us.

MR. CLAUSTROPHOBIA: You're right, Mrs. Calm. I'm sorry. You know, Bill, I'm lucky I got stuck in this elevator with Mrs. Calm because she's been a big help. She's been (5) _____ _____, trying to get me to calm down. All through this she has (6) _____. The truth is that she's absolutely great. Mrs. Calm, will you have dinner with me tonight if we ever get out of this elevator?

MRS. CALM: Why, Mr. Claustrophobia, it would be a pleasure. See, I told you that we'd (7) _____ this just fine.

5. Sentence Writing

Write three false sentences and one true sentence about yourself or your life for each group of expressions. Use any verb tense, and make some sentences negative. Read your sentences to your classmates. They will try to guess which sentence in each group is true. (*Variation:* Write three true sentences and one false sentence.)

Group 1	Group 2
out of the blue	make do
be better off	climb the walls
lose one's head	keep a level head
knock oneself out	be at the end of one's rope

6. Dictation

2,5

You will hear the dictation three times. First, just listen. Second, as you listen, write the dictation on a piece of paper. Skip lines. Third, check what you have written.

Key Words: scary, encouraged
Note: For *Mr. Claustrophobia*, write *Mr. C.*

7. Questions for Discussion and/or Writing

Discussion: You can answer these questions orally in groups or in the *Walk and Talk* activity in Appendix B.

Writing: You can write your own answers to these questions, or you can write the responses that you received from students during the *Walk and Talk* activity.

Questions

1. People from different cultural backgrounds may behave differently with strangers in places such as elevators. Some factors include the physical distance between them and whether or not they make eye contact or talk. In your native culture, how far do people usually stand from each other in crowded and uncrowded elevators? Do they make eye contact with each other? What do they look at? Do they talk to each other? On the street, do strangers smile at each other?

2. What are three to five events that can happen out of the blue and surprise people? Make a list.

3. Are people in your native country generally better off or worse off financially than they were twenty or thirty years ago? Explain.

4. When people don't have enough money to buy a lot of things, what are some things they do to "make do"?

5. What are some kinds of work that you have knocked yourself out doing?

8. Role Play or Write a Dialogue

In the cartoon, two people are climbing the stairs to the 12th floor in order to avoid taking the elevator that gave Mr. Claustrophobia so much trouble. They talk about what happened to Mr. Claustrophobia and their own fear of being stuck in an elevator.

Role play or write their conversation. Try to use some expressions from this lesson. Refer to or write on the board the list of expressions on page 103. Also, try to use other expressions that you know. But don't feel that it is necessary to have an idiom in every sentence.

Possible starting line: *I think we're better off taking the stairs than the elevator.*

9. Connection to the Real World

A. Culture and Language on the Internet

Web sites related to our lesson theme   Find information on the Internet about one or more of the following:

- various kinds of phobias.
- rules for how to behave on an elevator.

    Key words: *elevator etiquette* or *Miss Manners/elevator etiquette.*

- rules for how close or far people from different cultures stand from each other.

    Key words: *personal space, proximity.*

- the types of letters that Miss Manners and Dear Abby receive.

For the first three items above, informally in a group or formally in a short speech, report back to your class on some specific new information that you learned.

For the last item, look at some letters and tell a group or your class what kinds of topics Miss Manners and Dear Abby deal with. Choose one letter written to one of them, summarize it, and discuss how the columnist responded. Explain whether or not you agree with the advice.

Idiom Web site   In this lesson, you learned the expression *out of the blue.* Here are some more very common expressions with *out of.* Find out what they mean from an idiom Web site.

out of bounds	out of one's hands
out of breath	out of sight, out of mind
out of date	out of the ordinary
out of hand	out of the question
out of line	out of thin air

Euphemism Web site   A euphemism is a word or expression that people use to substitute for words that they don't want to say out loud. *For crying out loud* is a euphemism. Find a euphemism site on the Internet, and choose one euphemism to explain to a partner or group.

Quotation Web site   Mrs. Calm in this lesson shows that she is a very wise woman by the way she treats Mr. Claustrophobia. Find a quotation site on the Internet, and then search for quotes with the words *wisdom* or *wise.* See if you can find a quote that can be related to the way Mrs. Calm treated her companion.

Culture Note

In some cultures, people write letters to newspaper columnists regarding how to behave. In the United States, people often write to Dear Abby or Miss Manners. Is there a famous advice columnist that you know of?

Speech Instructions—
Appendix C

B. Contact Assignment

In this lesson, you learned phrasal verbs with **knock** and **come**. To learn more expressions with these words, with a partner ask a native speaker of English to help you fill out this chart. (For guidelines on how to do this kind of assignment, see Appendix F, "Contact Assignments," on page 197.)

Pronunciation Note: Remember to stress the second part of phrasal verbs.

		Meaning	Sample Sentence
knock			
	on	_____	_____
	it off	_____	_____
	over	_____	_____
come			
	about	_____	_____
	across	_____	_____
	to	_____	_____

10. Expression Collection

Every week, find three expressions from the real world that are new to you. Keep an inventory in your notebook or on index cards, following the format in Appendix G, "Expression Collection," on page 198. Be ready to share what you found in small groups or with your entire class.

Collocation Match-Up

Collocations are special combinations of words. Collocations can be idioms or other phrases and expressions. Find collocations from *Lessons 5 and 6* by matching the words from Column A with the words in Column B. Sometimes more than one answer is possible. (You will probably be able to make additional expressions that are not from Lessons 5 and 6. Put these in the box.)

A

  1. out of   _the blue_

  2. climb   _____

  3. better   _____

  4. cooped   _____

  5. sink   _____

  6. dwell   _____

  7. spilt   _____

  8. knock yourself   _____

  9. rule   _____

10. make the most   _____

11. worse   _____

12. haven't got   _____

13. sit   _____

14. be on the   _____

15. not have a   _____

16. down the   _____

17. the last   _____

18. come   _____

19. make   _____

20. up   _____

B

in

in the air

milk

tight

lookout

off

off

the blue √

drain

out

out

the walls

straw

clue

up

of

do

through

on

the slightest idea

Additional Collocations

Crossword Puzzle

Across

1 They need to take a walk. They have ___ fever.

6 What's ___ into them? They're acting crazy.

8 Everything is still up in ___ air.

10 Who knows what's in ___ for us in the future.

11 They didn't have much, but they ___ do with what they had.

13 He came ___ the surgery very well.

14 Yes. I'm sure beyond the ___ of a doubt.

18 His dog ate his homework. All his work went down the ___.

20 Come on. That's unheard ___!

21 I don't have the ___ idea where they went.

22 Listen, let's not ___ on what happened. Let's change the subject.

23 For ___ out loud, what did you do that for?

25 It's no ___ crying over spilt milk. You can't change what happened.

26 She appeared at our house out of the ___.

Down

2 Please don't leave me ___. I need someone to talk to.

3 Sit ___. I'll be there in a minute.

4 It's totally beyond my ___ how that could've happened.

5 She told me she's ___ the end of her rope.

7 I don't have any idea. Your ___ is as good as mine.

9 Don't panic. There is no point in your losing your ___.

11 Out of the corner of ___ eye, I could see something moving.

12 Getting stuck in the elevator was the last ___. He went nuts.

15 He knocked ___ out working on that assignment.

16 We'd be better ___ if we could start all over.

17 I'm not going to rule that ___. It's still possible.

19 It'll take some time for that news to ___ in.

23 I don't have a ___ about what he's talking about. Do you?

24 I've got to hand it to ___. You did a great job.

27 We don't want to be cooped ___ in that small house for three days.

NOW SHOWING

Violence in the Media—A Bone of Contention

Theme: Media Issues

Warm-Up

The subject of violence on TV, in movies, and in computer and video games has been discussed a great deal. Read the following quotations and indicate whether you agree or not. Discuss your reasons in a small group.

	Agree	Disagree	Not sure
1. Violence on TV does lead to aggressive behavior by children and teenagers.—*National Institute of Mental Health*			
2. The constant message . . . [is that] violence is the essential, appropriate, and inevitable means of solving all problems and settling all disputes.—*Alliance Against Violence in Entertaining for Children*			
3. Is there too much violent entertainment on TV? Absolutely. Is all violent entertainment on TV bad? Absolutely not.—Greg Dawson, *Orlando Sentinel*			
4. Just because a film has a murder scene doesn't mean people are going to commit the act. That overstates the power of the image and under-estimates the role of parents.—Psychiatrist Serge Tisseron			

Before You Listen

What is the difference in the people's expressions in the two cartoons on page 113? In the second cartoon, what do you think the people are discussing and why do you think their expressions changed?

As You Listen

(A) Close your book. Listen to the conversation between Angela and Jason to find the answers to these questions.

Who liked the movie, Angela or Jason?   What do they disagree about?

(B) Listen again, but this time read the conversation as you listen.

2,6

JASON:	So, what do you think?
ANGELA:	Well, **it's nothing to write home about.**
JASON:	You must be kidding!
ANGELA:	Why do you say that?
JASON:	I think it's the best movie I've seen in years!
ANGELA:	With all that violence?
JASON:	It wasn't so violent.
ANGELA:	It certainly was. There was blood in practically every scene. And sometimes the violence **had no bearing on** the story. It was just put in for audiences who like to see blood. I don't know how they can **get away with** showing so much detail . . .
JASON:	Well, **from my standpoint,** there was a real antiviolence message in the movie. They showed how all that violence ended in tragedy.
ANGELA:	But that's no excuse for being so graphic! Why did they have so many scenes with all that suffering?
JASON:	Because it was an important part of the story.
ANGELA:	Sorry, but that argument just **doesn't hold water.** You could cut some of those scenes out and still have your story. And **as far as** sending an antiviolence message, they can do that without making the audience sick.

JASON: Now you're really **blowing** this whole thing **out of proportion.**

ANGELA: Am I? Look at the crime statistics!

JASON: Listen, you know this subject is **a bone of contention** between us.
           We've had heated arguments about this kind of thing before.

ANGELA: Yes, too many. I sure hope that someday I'll **get through to** you.

JASON: All I know is I **got my money's worth** tonight.

ANGELA: Well, I'll agree that the story was engrossing, but all that blood and
           violence **drives me up the wall.**

JASON: Look, now we're back where we started. Let's just agree to disagree
           and go get a cup of coffee.

> engrossing = very interesting

After You Listen

(A) Read the sentences about the conversation. Circle *T* for *true*,
F for *false*, or *?* if you don't know.

1. Jason thinks the movie wasn't great, but that it was OK.   T (F) ?

2. Angela believes that the same story could have been
   told without all the violence.   (T) F ?

3. Children under 17 are not allowed to see this movie.   T F ?

4. This is the first time that Angela and Jason have had
   this kind of argument.   T (F) ?

5. Jason thinks Angela is exaggerating, and Angela hopes
   that she'll eventually convince Jason to agree with her.   (T) F ?

(B) **Guess the Meanings**
Below is a list of paraphrases of five of the idiomatic expressions
in the conversation. On your own or with a partner, try to guess
the five.

Paraphrase	Idiomatic Expression
1. it's nothing special	_____
2. convince	_____
3. a matter of disagreement	_____
4. had nothing to do with	_____
5. exaggerating	_____

(C) Say the conversation in pairs. Then have two students say the
conversation in front of the class.

Work with Others

If you're working with a partner or in a small group, read the short dialogues and examples for each expression aloud. Also, complete the Your Turn exercises together. Then, for each expression, circle *Yes* or *No* to show if you understand. If you circled *No*, highlight or underline what is unclear, and ask questions for clarification.

Figure It out on Your Own

Read the short dialogues and examples for each expression. Also complete the Your Turn exercises that don't need partners. Then, for each expression, circle *Yes* or *No* to show if you understand. If you circled *No*, highlight or underline what is still unclear, and ask questions in class for clarification.

ALL CLEAR ?

1. **(It's) nóthing to wríte HÓME about** = It's nothing special.

    Pronunciation Note: The word *home*, the last stressed word in this expression, should receive the highest intonation.

    A: I heard you ate at the new restaurant on the corner. How was it?
    B: The food's **nothing to write home about,** but the atmosphere is nice.

    Similar Expression: **léave a lót to be desíred** = not be adequate or satisfactory; not be as good as one would like.

    A: How was the movie?
    B: It **left a lot to be desired.** It was pretty boring.

Your Turn

Think about something that disappointed you—a trip, a movie, a restaurant, a course, etc. Then explain why it was nothing to write home about or why it left a lot to be desired.

2. **háve nó béaring on something** = have no connection to

ALL CLEAR ?
Yes No

A: The defense wanted to call her as a witness, but the judge wouldn't allow it. He said that her information **had no bearing on** the case.
B: So she didn't testify?
A: No, she didn't.

A: Why did you say that? It **has no bearing on** what we're talking about.
B: Yes it does. Let me explain.

Contrast: **lóse one's béarings** = become lost, lose one's sense of direction. (This can happen to anyone, but it especially happens to people with Alzheimer's disease.)

A: Please don't let my grandmother go out alone. She always **loses her bearings.**
B: Don't worry. I'll be with her every minute.

3. **get awáy with something** = succeed in doing something undesirable or illegal without being caught or punished

ALL CLEAR ?
Yes No

Grammar Note: When you want to use a verb after this expression, turn it into a gerund.

A: Those kids always **get away with** do**ing** whatever they want.
B: That's because their parents don't set any limits.

A: I wonder if I'll **get away with** turn**ing** in my friend's paper from two years ago. Do you think the teacher will remember it?
B: Who knows? Is it worth it to you? Wouldn't you feel guilty? You know that would be cheating.

Contrast: **get awáy with múrder** = do something very bad and not be caught or punished. This is a general expression—it doesn't specifically state what someone is getting away with.

A: Do you see what those kids are doing? They're practically destroying the house!
B: That's nothing new. Their parents always let them **get away with murder.**

Your Turn

Do you know anyone who got away with cheating on a test or cheating in another way at school? What happened?

ALL CLEAR ?

4. **from someone's stándpoint** = from someone's **point of view** = in someone's opinion

Pronunciation Note: Stress the possessive adjective in this expression to emphasize whose opinion is being given: From MY standpoint, . . .

- Your position is very clear. But **from my standpoint,** you have come to the wrong conclusion because you haven't got all the necessary information.
- **From his standpoint,** parents should be responsible for what their kids watch on TV and see in the movies and on the Internet.

ALL CLEAR ?

5. **something dóesn't hóld wáter** = something (an explanation, a belief, etc.) is not strong and would not be able to be supported

A: The suspect's alibi that he was home at the time of the murder **doesn't hold water.**

B: Why not?

A: Because the police found out from the neighbors that he left home at 9:30 and didn't get back till after 11:00.

A: I'm sorry, but your argument **doesn't hold water.** TV does affect kids' behavior.

B: Can you give me an example?

A: Sure. Don't you remember the story about the little boy who jumped off a building, thinking he could fly like Superman?

2,7

Your Turn: Listening Challenge

Listen to the conversation. Find out why the woman's argument doesn't hold water.

The woman's argument doesn't hold water because _____

_____

6. **as fár as (something is concerned)** = in regard to, related to something

ALL CLEAR ?

Grammar Note: Use a noun or gerund after **as far as.**

A: How do you keep your kids from seeing violence on TV, in the movies, and on the Internet?

B: Well, we just don't let them watch certain programs on TV and we let them see movies that are only rated G or PG. **As far as** (OR: **As far as using**) the Internet, that's a bigger problem and we're working on that.

Common Expressions with "as far as":

As fár as I knów, = What I know is that . . .

A: Where are they?

B: **As far as I know,** they went on vacation.

As fár as Í'm concérned, = in my opinion, . . .

A: How did you like the movie?

B: **As far as I'm concerned,** it was a big disappointment.

Culture Note

The Motion Picture Association of America (MPAA) has a movie rating system and parental guidelines for TV programs to help parents know if material is appropriate for children. Are rating systems used in your native country?

7. **blów something óut of propórtion** = exaggerate the importance of something

ALL CLEAR ?

A: Why is your sister so upset with you?

B: Because I told her that her sweater didn't look good on her, and she **blew it out of proportion.** She said that I'm always criticizing her. And all I was talking about was her sweater, nothing else.

A: OK, I'll start the whole project over again.

B: Wait a minute. Don't **blow this out of proportion.** I didn't say that you needed to redo the whole thing. I just said that you need to work more on one part of it.

8. **a bóne of conténtion (between)** = something to argue or fight about

Origin: A bone of contention would literally be a bone that two dogs fight over.

A: When we're with them, don't bring up the subject of prayer in public schools.

B: Why not?

A: You know we've always disagreed on that. It's a **bone of contention between** us, and I want to avoid it.

• Let's not talk about politics. You know it's a **bone of contention between** us, and I don't feel like getting into a debate.

9. **get thróugh to someone** = reach someone with ideas

A: How can I **get through to** you? Why won't you believe me?

B: It's not that I don't believe you. It's just that I don't agree with you.

A: Did you get him to change his mind about dropping out of school?

B: I tried, but I couldn't **get through to** him.

Contrast the telephone meaning of **get through (to someone)**:

A: Have you reached them yet?

B: No. I've been trying for an hour, but I can't **get through** (to them).

A: Have you tried their cell phone?

10. **gét one's móney's wórth (out of something)** = get the value of what one has paid for

   A: I didn't know you got a new computer.
   B: Yeah, a few months ago. But I've been having a lot of problems with it and I'm going to take it back and tell them I **didn't get my money's worth.** They have to fix it or give me another one.

   A: Our trip was expensive, but we sure **got our money's worth out of it.**
   B: That's good news. Why was it so great?
   A: Well, everything was perfect. We stayed in a beautiful place and got a lot of rest. We went to the beach, ate out, went dancing . . .

Your Turn

What is the most expensive thing you bought during this past year? Did you get your money's worth? Explain.

11. **drive someone up the wáll = drive someone crázy = drive someone núts =** cause someone to feel angry, uncomfortable, or crazy

   A: Have you read his new book?
   B: No. His ideas **drive me up the wall.**

   • Can you change the station? That music **drives me up the wall.**

Your Turn

What drives you up the wall at home? At school? At work? In this country? Why?

NEW EXPRESSION COLLECTION

It's nothing to write home about.	from my standpoint	a bone of contention
a lot to be desired	from my point of view	get through to
no bearing on	doesn't hold water	get my money's worth
lose his bearings	as far as	drives me up the wall
get away with (murder)	blow (it) out of proportion	

(See page 168 for pronunciation exercises for Lesson 7.)

2,8

1. Mini-Dialogues

Read the sentences in Column A. Choose the *best* response from Column B. Not all responses can be used. Then say each mini-dialogue with a partner.

1A	1B
_d_ **1.** I lost my job, so my life is over.	**a.** OK. We'll stay home.
_a_ **2.** Money has no bearing on my decision. I just don't want to go.	**b.** I know what you mean. They let them get away with murder.
_f_ **3.** How was the movie?	**c.** I tried, but I can't get through.
_b_ **4.** I don't like to have them over because their kids drive me up the wall.	**d.** Don't say that. You're blowing it out of proportion.
_e_ **5.** As far as I'm concerned, you need to get your facts straight. Your argument just doesn't hold water.	**e.** Well, from my standpoint, everything makes sense. I can't see why you disagree.
	f. It was nothing to write home about. But dinner was great.

2A	2B
_c_ **1.** They didn't get away with cheating. Their teacher caught them.	**a.** It left a lot to be desired.
_d_ **2.** When the old man lost his bearings, someone helped him out.	**b.** There's no doubt about it. I learned a lot, and it helped me get a better job.
_e_ **3.** In his family, the subject of politics is a bone of contention, so they try to avoid it.	**c.** Good for her!
_b_ **4.** It sounds like you really got your money's worth out of that course.	**d.** That doesn't happen often enough. We need more people like that.
_f_ **5.** As far as going back there again, I don't know. It wasn't anything to write home about.	**e.** Oh, really? We like to have heated arguments around the dinner table.
	f. Why? What happened? Did you have a bad time?

2. Grammar Practice

Follow the directions and complete the sentences.

Directions	**Sentences**
1. Add a preposition.	a. We can't get through _____ her. She doesn't listen. b. What you said has no bearing _____ what happened. c. Those little kids get away _____ murder. d. _____ his standpoint, we're wrong. e. _____ his point _____ view, we're wrong. f. You're blowing this out _____ proportion. g. That's a bone _____ contention _____ them. h. The movie was nothing to write home _____. i. We sure got our money's worth out _____ that TV!
2. Add a gerund.	a. In this school, students don't get away with _____. b. As far as _____ here forever, I'm not sure.
3. Use past tense.	a. It wasn't so great. It _____ a lot to be desired. b. They _____ their bearings in the snow, but they were rescued after a few hours. c. He got angry and said that she _____ everything out of proportion. d. The music at that party _____ me crazy. e. He lost the debate because his argument _____ water.

3. Error Correction

Find the errors and make corrections. Some sentences have two errors. One item is correct.

1. The conference wasn't so great. It left a lot to write home about.

2. When I walked out of the building, I turned right and lose my bearing.

3. You need to take this paragraph out of your essay. It has no bearing on your topic.

4. She thinks she can get away with turn in her homework late all the time, but she's going to have a big surprise.

5. In my point of view, he's getting away with murder.

6. The jury said his argument didn't held water, so they decided that he was guilty.

7. As far as buy a new car, I think we need to wait and save more money.

8. When I told her that the chicken wasn't cooked enough, she blow it out proportion and said that she was a failure, that she couldn't do anything right.

9. When we couldn't get through them for two days, we drove over to their apartment to make sure they were OK.

10. **A:** Why did you leave so early?

    B: Because the music was drive me nuts.

2,9

4. Choosing the Idiom

The following is a letter to a newspaper advice columnist from a man named Jess. Jess is complaining about his roommate and looking for advice. Fill in the blanks with the best possible expressions from the list. Pay special attention to how the expressions are used grammatically. You may need to consider verb tenses, subject-verb agreement, pronouns, active vs. passive voice, etc. Not all of the expressions can be used. After you finish, practice reading the sentences aloud.

get through to	as far as	leave a lot to be desired
from my standpoint	get away with murder	drive me up the wall
have no bearing on	blow things out of proportion	get one's money's worth
bone of contention		

Dear Prudence,

I just got a new roommate who (1) _____.
(2) _____, he's extremely inconsiderate. He leaves his stuff all over the apartment and doesn't care if it bothers me. I imagine that when he was a kid, his parents let him (3) _____. When I complained to him about the mess, he told me that my cooking (4) _____ _____ and that (5) _____ _____ he was concerned, I wasn't a very good roommate for him. And please don't even ask me about washing dishes around here. That's a big (6) _____ _____ between us. I don't want to (7) _____, but things are really terrible and I'm thinking about asking him to move out. Or maybe I'll move out. Can you give me any advice about how I can (8) _____ _____ him and get him to change?

Jess in a Mess

5. Sentence Writing

Write three false sentences and one true sentence about yourself or your life for the group of expressions. Use any verb tense, and make some sentences negative. Read your sentences to your classmates. They will try to guess which sentence is true. (*Variation:* Write three true sentences and one false sentence.)

get away with murder	a bone of contention between
from my standpoint	drive me up the wall

6. Dictation

You will hear the dictation three times. First, just listen. Second, as you listen, write the dictation on a piece of paper. Skip lines. Third, check what you have written.

2,10

Key Words: violence, violent, accused

7. Questions For Discussion and/or Writing

Discussion: You can answer these questions orally in groups or in the *Walk and Talk* activity in Appendix B.

Writing: You can write your own answers to these questions, or you can write the responses that you received from students during the *Walk* and *Talk* activity.

Questions

1. Think about when you were a child. Do you remember any particular instance when something you saw in the movies or on TV really scared you? Do you think having experiences like this is good or bad for children?

2. Have you heard of any problems that have come up when children have gone on the Internet and participated in chat room discussions? How do you think parents and others can protect children from dangers on the Internet?

3. When you were a child, did your parents let you get away with murder, or were they strict? Explain.

4. From your standpoint, how should parents discipline their children—with words or by striking them physically?

5. The news media are often accused of blowing stories out of proportion. In other words, they may take a story and make it sound more important than it really is. What do you think? (If possible, give examples from the news.)

6. Give an example of a bone of contention between you and someone you know. Or, if you'd rather not get too personal, give an example of a bone of contention between two people that you know.

8. Role Play or Write a Dialogue

In the cartoon, Angela and Jason are talking at a cafe after the movie. Even though they "agreed to disagree" about the movie, they continue to have a heated discussion about other topics (possibly political issues, their differing opinions of friends or relatives, certain kinds of music or sports, etc.).

Role play or write their conversation. Try to use some expressions from this lesson. Refer to or write on the board the list of expressions on page 121. Also, try to use other expressions that you know. But don't feel that it is necessary to have an idiom in every sentence.

Possible starting line: *I can't wait for tomorrow to see the big game on TV.*

9. Connection to the Real World

A. Culture and Language on the Internet

Web sites related to our lesson theme Find information on the Internet about how parents can try to control what their children see and hear on TV, in movies, in music, or on the Internet. Key words: *media violence, parent control, movie ratings, Motion Picture Association of America (MPAA)*.

- Informally in a group or formally in a short speech, report back to your class on some specific new information that you learned.

Speech Instructions— Appendix C

OR

- Take roles and conduct a panel discussion on whether or not media violence causes children and others to be violent in real life and whether or not governments should have a part in controlling what is produced. Possible roles: psychologist, parent, teenager, TV producer, police officer. Look for information on the Internet that you might use in your role on the panel. Key words: *media violence, children, debate, freedom of speech*.

Panel Discussion— Appendix D

OR

- If you are at a school where there is a psychology or education department, invite a teacher from that department to talk to your class about media violence and its effects on children. Listen, take notes, and ask the speaker questions.

Guest Speaker— Appendix E

Idiom Web Site/Proverb Web Site

- In this lesson, you learned the expressions *It's nothing to write home about* and *It doesn't hold water.* Here are some more expressions with home and water. Find out what they mean from an idiom website.

Home	**Water**
bring home the bacon	be in hot water
eat somebody out of house and home	water down
hit home	make your mouth water
until the cows come home	water under the bridge

- Visit a proverb Web site and search for proverbs with the words *home* or *water*.

Quotation Web Site/Urban Legend Web Site

- Find a quotation site on the Internet, and then search for (a) quotes with the words *media violence* and *gratuitous violence*. Also search for quotes related to *freedom of speech*. (b) For fun, search for *movie quotes* or *funny quotes*.

- Search the Internet for *urban legends*. Find out what urban legends are, and find examples of *movies* or *TV*.

B. Contact Assignment

In this lesson, you learned the phrasal verbs **get through to** and **get away with.** To learn more expressions with **get,** with a partner ask a native speaker of English to help you fill out this chart. (For guidelines on how to do this kind of assignment, see Appendix F, "Contact Assignments," on page 197.)

Pronunciation Note: Remember to stress the second part of phrasal verbs.

get	Meaning	Sample Sentence
ahead	_____	_____
at	_____	_____
around to	_____	_____
back at	_____	_____
even with	_____	_____
down to	_____	_____
on with	_____	_____

10. Expression Collection

Every week, find three expressions from the real world that are new to you. Keep an inventory in your notebook or on index cards, following the format in Appendix G, "Expression Collection," on page 198. Be ready to share what you found in small groups or with your entire class.

Changing Time Zones—A Bad Case of Jet Lag

Theme: Traveling

Warm-Up

Read the following explanation of *jet lag,* offered by Professor Karl C. Hamner of UCLA: "After travelers fly across many time zones in a day, they are under new local times, and it takes a few days for their bodies to adjust to the new day-night patterns. This phenomenon is commonly called *jet lag.*"

Answer the following:

Have you ever taken a long airplane trip? If yes, tell your classmates:

- where you started from and landed.
- what the time difference is between where you took off from and where you landed.
- whether or not you took naps at unusual times or were awake in the middle of the night soon after your arrival.
- how long it took you to adjust to the time in the country you arrived in.
- your advice for travelers on how to prevent or get over jet lag.

Focused Listening

Before You Listen

Look at the cartoons on page 129, and use your imagination to answer these questions: Where do you think the young woman just returned from? What could she have been doing there? Why are they taking a walk?

As You Listen

(A) Close your book. Listen to the conversation between the father and daughter to find the answers to these questions.

What was the daughter doing in another country?
What good things did she experience?

(B) Listen again, but this time read the conversation as you listen.

2,11

(at home)

DAUGHTER: Dad, what time is it?

FATHER: Four.

DAUGHTER: Four? Who knows what time that is for me! Boy, I **have** terrible **jet lag. I can't keep my eyes open.**

FATHER: Well, I'm not going to let you go to sleep in the middle of the afternoon. Let's take a walk, and you can tell me about your trip.

DAUGHTER: I'm sorry Daddy, but **I'm** too **wiped out.** I think I'll **stretch out** and take a little nap.

FATHER: Uh-uh—no naps. You know if you go to sleep now, you're going to wake up in the middle of the night. Come on, let's take a little walk around the block. Maybe you'll **get a second wind.**

DAUGHTER: I sure hope so.

(on their walk)

DAUGHTER: I missed you and Mom a lot. A year is a long time.

FATHER: We missed you too, honey. But we knew that studying in another country was good for you.

DAUGHTER: Well, I sure **had my ups and downs.** Sometimes I even thought about coming home early, but I was determined to stick it out.*

*See Lesson 3

FATHER: And I'm glad you did. But you didn't tell us you were having problems. What was so hard for you over there?

DAUGHTER: Oh, I don't think I can **scratch the surface.** There were times, especially in the winter, when I got really homesick. You know, it's hard to be away during holidays. But my friends were absolutely great. Especially my roommate. Remember she took me home to her family? That really helped.

FATHER: If we'd known how homesick you were, we would've **hopped on** a plane! Why didn't you let us know?

DAUGHTER: Oh, I didn't want you to worry. And it would've been too expensive. Anyway, in the spring I got much better. **It** finally **hit home** that I was lucky to be living in another culture. I stopped thinking so much about my problems and **got out of my rut.** I started going to more parties and concerts and things like that. And listen to this! After a while, I didn't realize it, but my fluency improved. Can you imagine that there were times when I forgot I wasn't speaking English?

FATHER: Wow! **That's music to my ears!** I knew you'd do it if you lived over there.

DAUGHTER: And **to top that off,** people started to compliment my pronunciation.

FATHER: You don't want to lose all that, honey. Are there any conversation classes you can take here?

DAUGHTER: Uh—Dad, I wasn't going to **broach the subject** till later, but . . . there's a chance that I can get a scholarship and go back next year.

FATHER: Go back? But you just got home!

DAUGHTER: I know.

FATHER: Do you really want to go back?

DAUGHTER: The truth is, I'm not sure. I need to **sleep on it.** Speaking of sleep, now can I take a little nap? I'm so sleepy!

After You Listen

(A) Read the sentences about the conversation. Circle *T* for *true*, *F* for *false*, or *?* if you don't know.

1. The father and daughter took a walk so she wouldn't fall asleep.   **T** F ?

2. When the daughter was away, she told her parents that she was very homesick.   **T** F ?

3. In the spring, she realized how lucky she was to have the opportunity to live in another country.   **T** F ?

4. She stopped going to parties and started studying more.   T **F** ?

5. She's going to take a conversation class so she can continue to speak the foreign language that she learned.   T F **?**

(B) **Guess the Meanings**

Below is a list of paraphrases of five of the idiomatic expressions in the conversation. On your own or with a partner, try to guess the five.

Paraphrase	Idiomatic Expression
1. had good times and bad times	up and down
2. lie down	stretch out
3. mention the topic	
4. gotten on	hopped on
5. I finally realized	hit home

(C) Say the conversation in pairs. Then have two students say the conversation in front of the class.

Understanding the New Expressions

Work with Others

If you're working with a partner or in a small group, read the short dialogues and examples for each expression aloud. Also, complete the Your Turn exercises together. Then, for each expression, circle *Yes* or *No* to show if you understand. If you circled *No*, highlight or underline what is unclear, and ask questions for clarification.

Figure It out on Your Own

Read the short dialogues and examples for each expression. Also complete the Your Turn exercises that don't need partners. Then, for each expression, circle *Yes* or *No* to show if you understand. If you circled *No*, highlight or underline what is still unclear, and ask questions in class for clarification.

1. **(have) jét lag** = feel sleepy during the day and awake at night because your body is used to a different time zone

   Other verbs used with this expression: **avoid/prevent/get over jet lag**

   A: Do you know how I can **avoid jet lag?**
   B: Well, some people try to change the time they go to bed before they travel, but I don't know if that works.

   A: You're landing on Sunday and going to work on Monday? How is that possible? Won't you **have jet lag?**
   B: Probably, but I can do it. I usually **get over jet lag** pretty fast.

2. **cán't kéep one's éyes ópen** = can't stay awake because one is so sleepy

   A: It's time to put the kids to bed. Look—**they can't keep their eyes open.**
   B: You're right. . . . Come on, kids, bedtime!

3. **be wiped óut** = be very, very tired; be exhausted

   Note: This is a very informal expression.

   A: I'**m wiped out.** I spent six hours on this assignment!
   B: I'd **be wiped out** too.

   Contrast the literal meaning of **"wípe out:"** clean (wipe/rub) the inside of something, usually with a cloth
   • I **wiped out** the sink.

4. stretch óut = lie down

- I'm going to **stretch out** on the couch and take a nap.
- This couch isn't very long. You can't **stretch out.**

Note: This phrasal verb cannot be separated. Don't put any words between *stretch out.*

Contrast: **stretch something óut** = make something wider or longer

- Look at how far you can **stretch out** this rubber band.
- He **stretched** the story **out** with millions of details. I almost fell asleep.

Contrast: **be stretched óut**

A: Look! My sweater **is** all **stretched out.**
B: Did you put it in the washing machine?
A: Uh-huh.
B: That's why. You should've washed it by hand.

5. gét a sécond wínd = get new energy after being very tired

Origin Note: An athlete, such as a runner, may breathe very fast at first. When the breathing becomes regular again, it is called a *second wind.*

A: What are you doing? I thought you said you were too tired to clean the house.
B: I don't know. Somehow **I got a second wind.**

A: I'm full of energy. It's weird, because an hour ago I needed a nap.
B: You **got a second wind.** But I didn't. I'm going to take a break.

Your Turn

Tell a partner about a time when you were so wiped out that you couldn't keep your eyes open. Did you get a second wind?

6. **háve one's úps and dówns** = have good and bad periods of time

ALL CLEAR ?

A: How's your new job?
B: It **has its ups and downs,** but it's all right.

A: How is she now that she's back home?
B: She **has her ups and downs** just like she does everywhere else.

7. **scrátch the súrface** = talk or write about a topic on a superficial level; not go deeply into the subject

ALL CLEAR ?

Pronunciation Note: pronounce 'face' in the word *surface* as 'iss' —> 'surfiss.'

Opposite: **in dépth** = talk or write about a topic completely or deeply

- I've told you a little about my trip. But I only **scratched the surface** because there's so much more to tell.
- When they've finished this course, many students think they've learned all there is to know about this subject. But I'm afraid that we can only **scratch the surface** here. There's so much more to learn, and we can't cover it all.
- You've only **scratched the surface** of the environmental problems we face. We need to continue this conversation and discuss each problem **in depth.**

8. **hóp on** = get on a plane, bus, train, motorcycle, or boat without much planning beforehand

ALL CLEAR ?

Similar Expression: **hop ín** (a car)
This expression is usually used in the imperative form: *Hop in!*

Note: These are informal expressions that are used to show that someone gets on a means of transportation somewhat spontaneously, without much planning.

Pronunciation Note: When you just say "Hop *on!*" or "Hop *in,*" stress the second word.

A: (on the phone): I need you. Can you come right away?
B: Absolutely! I'll **hop on** the next plane/train/bus.

A: When I heard what happened, I **hopped on** the first plane I could get.
B: I'm sure they felt better when you got there.

A: (talking through a car window to friends): Can I join you?
B: Sure, **hop in!**

9. **it hít hóme (that)** = something finally became clear deep in one's heart or mind

- They knew they'd won the lottery, but it didn't really **hit home** until they got their first check and bought a new car.
- When it finally **hit home** that they were going to be parents, they got a little scared.
- It finally **hit home** that she had lost her job when she woke up and had nowhere to go.

Similar Expression: **it (finally) hit someone that** = something made someone realize that . . .

It finally **hit him that**

- he was really a father.
- she was not a little girl anymore, that she had grown up.
- he had to work harder or he'd lose his job.
- he would never see them again.

Your Turn

Think of a time when it took you a while to really believe something. With a partner, complete the following. Use the sentences above as models.

1. _____, but it didn't really

   hit home until _____.

2. When it finally hit home that _____,

   _____.

3. It finally hit home that _____

   when _____.

4. It finally hit me that _____.

10. **gét out of one's rút** = get out of an unhappy psychological situation or boring routine

Note: A *rut* is literally a track below the level of the ground that can cause one to get stuck

ALL CLEAR ?

A: I need to **get out of this rut.** I need a big change from this boring routine.

B: Why don't you look for another job or take a class?

Contrast: **be in a rút**

A: Do you know why he always looks so unhappy?

B: He seems to **be in a rut.** I think he needs a change, or at least a vacation.

A: You seem much happier than you were the last time I saw you.

B: Yeah, I'm better. I **was in a rut** then, but I've made some changes, and things are much better now.

11. **músic to one's éars** = great news that is a pleasure to hear

ALL CLEAR ?

A: Mom, we're moving back home. We want the kids to grow up near you and Dad. They need to grow up near their grandparents.

B: Oh, honey . . . that's **music to my ears!**

• When she said "I love you," it was **music to his ears.**

Contrast: **be áll éars** = be ready and eager to listen

A: Do you want to hear about my trip?

B: Yes, I've been waiting. I**'m all ears.**

A: Wait till you hear what happened!

B: Hurry up and tell us. We**'re all ears.**

Your Turn

Think about the difference between these two idioms. Complete the dialogs and then say them with a partner.

A: _____

B: That's music to my ears!

A: _____

B: I'm all ears.

ALL CLEAR ?

hors d'oeuvres = appetizers

12. **to top thát off, . . .** = To add to what I have already said, here is one more thing that makes what happened before either better or worse.

Note: First you say what happened, and then you add what was unexpected.

A: First we met at my house and had some hors d'oeuvres. Then we went to a really nice restaurant, and after that we went to the theater. And **to top that all off,** we went out for drinks afterward.

B: Wow! What an evening!

A: My car was stolen, I lost my books, and **to top that off,** I caught a cold.

B: Poor kid. Your luck will change.

Your Turn

Complete the sentences.

1. It was the best night of my life. We had front row seats at the concert. We sat next to some famous rock musicians. And to top that off,

    _____!

2. It was the worst night of my life. First, the concert was canceled. Then, I had an argument with my friends. And to top that off,

    _____!

ALL CLEAR ?

13. **bróach the súbject** = introduce a new topic while feeling that the response from others may be negative

Note: Because a negative response is expected when someone *broaches a subject,* people often start sentences with phrases such as: *I wasn't going to . . . ; I was afraid to . . . ; I hate to . . . ; I know you don't want me to . . . .*

Origin Note: An instrument called a *broach* is used to open beer barrels. When the barrels are opened, the beer is brought to light, just as a subject has been brought to light when it is broached (brought up). *(Source: Brewer's Dictionary of Phrase & Fable)*

A: Did you ask?
B: No. I was afraid to **broach the subject** because they were upset.

- I hate to **broach the subject** of money right now, but can I borrow a few dollars?
- I know you don't want me to **broach the subject,** but when are you going to get married? You're not getting any younger.

Similar Expression: **bring úp (a subject), bring (something) úp** = introduce a new topic. This expression is neutral—the response from others may or may not be negative. (The response when "broaching a subject" is expected to be negative.)

A: I need to **bring up** another **subject** before the meeting is over. Do you think we'll have time?
B: Sure. What's it about?

A: We need to talk about salaries.
B: I'm glad you **brought** that **up.** I almost forgot.

14. sléep on it = not make a decision quickly; think about something and make a decision the next day or even later

ALL CLEAR ?

A: Will you marry me?
B: Uh—
A: Don't answer me now. **Sleep on it** and let me know tomorrow.

A: Will you take the new job?
B: I can't say yet. I need to **sleep on it** for a few days.

A: It's a great chance for a vacation. Should I make the reservations?
B: I don't know . . . Can I **sleep on it** and tell you tomorrow?

- I **slept on it,** and yes, I will marry you!
- She **slept on it** and decided not to take the new job.
- I **slept on it** and decided that you should go ahead and make those reservations. It sounds like a great idea for a vacation.

Your Turn: Listening Challenge

Imagine that Michael and Nancy are asking you for advice about career opportunities. Listen to each of them, and then talk about what you think they should do.

2,12

I think Michael should . . . because . . . .
I think Nancy should . . . because . . . .

Exercises

(See page 173 for pronunciation exercises for Lesson 8.)

2,13

1. Mini-Dialogues

Read the sentences in Column A. Choose the *best* response from Column B. Not all responses can be used. Then say each mini-dialogue with a partner.

1A	1B
___ **1.** I thought you were tired.	**a.** I'm all ears.
___ **2.** Can I tell you a secret?	**b.** It's all stretched out.
___ **3.** I think I'll stretch out and read for a while.	**c.** That's for sure. They usually just scratch the surface of the stories.
___ **4.** I heard he got out of the hospital. How's he doing?	**d.** Well, he has his ups and downs.
___ **5.** They rarely give the news in depth.	**e.** I was, but I got a second wind, and now I'm full of energy.
___ **6.** I'm sorry, I can't decide right now.	**f.** There's a lounge chair outside. I think you'll be very comfortable there.
	g. No problem. Sleep on it and then give me a call

2A	2B
___ **1.** You've been studying night and day. What's going on?	**a.** Great. I'm not as wiped out as I thought I'd be.
___ **2.** How was your twenty-hour trip?	**b.** And to top it off, we bought two new cars!
___ **3.** We're getting married.	**c.** That's music to my ears!
___ **4.** Can you give me a ride home?	**d.** I'm afraid to broach the subject, but can I borrow a few bucks?
___ **5.** I'm moving across the country. I need to get out of this rut.	**e.** What about your family? Are you going to just pick up and go?
___ **6.** What's wrong?	**f.** After I got a low grade on my last test, it finally hit home that I have to get more serious about school.
	g. Sure. Hop in.

2. Grammar Practice

Follow the directions and complete the sentences.

	Directions	Sentences
1.	Add an article.	a. The kids were tired, but then they got _____ second wind. b. Let's talk some more. We've only just scratched _____ surface. c. I don't want to broach _____ subject, but I have to. d. He was in _____ rut, but he's OK now because he went back to school.
2.	Add a preposition.	a. Let's talk about this _____ depth. b. Do you need a ride? Hop _____! c. If you hop _____ a plane, you'll be there in a few hours. d. You got the job? That's music _____ my ears. e. I can't decide now. I have to sleep _____ it.
3.	Use idioms with different verb tenses.	a. I'm going to bring up the subject later. He _____ up the subject yesterday. b. You slept on it yesterday. I _____ on it tonight. c. She had her ups and downs when she got home. She _____ her ups and downs since she got home. d. Tell us. We're all ears. We _____ all ears when he told us.

3. Error Correction

Find the errors and make corrections. Some sentences have two errors. One item is correct.

1. When the teacher saw that he can't keep her eyes open, she didn't know if he was tired, or if the class was boring.

2. He was so wipe out that he fell asleep in class.

3. I think I'll stretch myself out for a few minutes.

4. That ten-year-old kid's a genius. He can do advanced math, and he knows college-level chemistry. To top that off, he can speak nine languages!

5. My uncle is 95! He has his up and down, but he's OK.

6. Everyone was getting tired before the break, but then we all get second wind.

7. When I got out of the plane, it hits me that I was really there.

8. Did you make your decision? You said you would slept on it.

9. She's in rut. She needs a change in her routine.

10. A: Did you talk about it when you saw her?

    B: No, I didn't brought up it because she was in a hurry.

2,14

4. Choosing the Idiom

The following is a conversation between the daughter from the introductory conversation and her mother. Her mother is trying to wake her up from her nap. Fill in the blanks with the best possible expressions from the list. Pay special attention to how the expressions are used grammatically. You may need to consider verb tenses, subject-verb agreement, pronouns, active vs. passive voice, etc. Not all of the expressions can be used. After you finish, practice reading the sentences aloud.

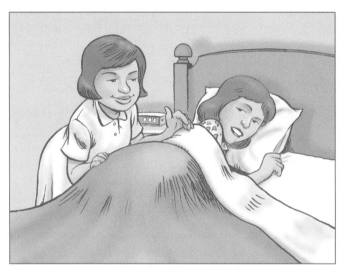

have one's ups and downs   get a second wind
to top that off   get over jet lag
scratch the surface   hop on
it hit home   wiped out
be all ears   hop in

MOTHER: Honey, wake up. Come on.

DAUGHTER: What time is it?

MOTHER: It's almost 7:00. You need to get ready for dinner.

DAUGHTER: I'm not hungry, Mom. Please let me sleep. I'm so
(1) _____.

MOTHER: But you'll never (2) _____
if you keep taking naps. Come on. Maybe you'll (3) _____
_____ after you have
something to eat.

DAUGHTER: I doubt it. Please let me rest for a few more minutes.

MOTHER: OK. Just a few minutes. Why don't you tell me about your plans. Dad told me that you might go back next year, and to tell you the truth, I want you to stay home and finish school here. We missed you so much when you were away.

DAUGHTER: I missed you, too.

MOTHER: On your birthday I almost (4) _____ _____ a plane to visit you. I wanted to surprise you.

DAUGHTER: You should've come. I would've introduced you to all my friends.

MOTHER: Tell me about them now. I (5) _____ _____.

DAUGHTER: Now? I'm too tired. How can I even (6) _____ _____? There's so much to tell.

MOTHER: Well, you can start at the dinner table.

DAUGHTER: Dinner, dinner, dinner.

MOTHER: Aha! Now you're awake!

DAUGHTER: Please let's just talk here. I don't want to get up. But *you* talk. Tell me about how *you've* been.

MOTHER: Well, you know, when you first left, it was so quiet around here. (7) _____ that you were really on your own. My baby had left the nest. It was hard at the beginning not having any kids around. One day I'd be fine, and the next day I'd be kind of sad. I guess I (8) _____ But over time I got better. Hey! Your eyes are closing. Kate! Don't go back to sleep!

5. Sentence Writing

Write three false sentences and one true sentence about yourself or your life for each group of expressions. Use any verb tense, and make some sentences negative. Read your sentences to your classmates. They will try to guess which sentence in each group is true. (*Variation:* Write three true sentences and one false sentence.)

Group 1	**Group 2**
get over jet lag	sleep on it
couldn't keep my eyes open	bring up (a subject)
stretch out	scratch the surface
broach the subject	be wiped out

6. Dictation

2,15

You will hear the dictation three times. First, just listen. Second, as you listen, write the dictation on a piece of paper. Skip lines. Third, check what you have written.

Key Words: awake, suggested, opportunity, abroad

7. Questions for Discussion and/or Writing

Discussion: You can answer these questions orally in groups or in the *Walk and Talk* activity in Appendix B.

Writing: You can write your own answers to these questions, or you can write the responses that you received from students during the *Walk* and *Talk* activity.

Questions

1. Do you think young people should live with their parents until they get married? Or, do you think it's good for young people to move out of their parents' home at around 18 and learn to be independent? Explain.

2. Have you ever had jet lag? If yes, where were you? What did you do to stay awake? If you were awake when everyone else was sleeping, what did you do?

3. If you are living in a foreign culture, or if you have ever lived in a foreign culture, describe some of the ups and downs that you have experienced.

4. What are one or two subjects that you'd like to learn about in depth? Be specific and explain why a subject interests you. (Possible subjects: history, politics, psychology, education, care of children, care of the elderly, space research, the environment, linguistics.)

5. Have you or someone you know ever been in a rut (e.g., unhappy in a job/depressed because of a boring routine)? If yes, what was the problem? Talk about ways to get out of a rut.

8. Role Play or Write a Dialogue

In the cartoon, Martha and Tony have just arrived in another country for a conference. They are talking in the hotel lobby. The opening session (meeting) will take place in two hours, but Martha and Tony aren't sure that they have enough energy to go after their long trip.

Role play or write their conversation. Try to use some expressions from this lesson. Refer to or write on the board the list of expressions on page 140. Also, try to use other expressions that you know. But don't feel that it is necessary to have an idiom in every sentence.

Possible starting lines: *Do you think you have enough energy to go to the opening session? Do you know what time it is at home right now?*

9. Connection to the Real World

A. Culture and Language on the Internet

Web sites related to our lesson theme Find information on the Internet about one or more of the following topics related to traveling:

- jet lag (ways to prevent it; how to get over it)
- culture shock
- reverse culture shock
- stereotypes of people from different cultures

Informally in a group or formally in a short speech, report back to your class on some specific new information that you learned.

Role play a panel discussion. Have three students each take the role of student adviser. The panel is preparing an audience of students that will be leaving for another country to study for one year. One adviser will talk about how to try to prevent and how to get over jet lag. One adviser will talk about culture shock. And the other adviser will talk about the dangers of stereotyping. The advisers will present their advice, and members of the audience will ask questions. (*Variation:* Three advisers talk to an audience of business people who are going to work in another country for one year.)

Idiom Web site In this lesson, you learned the expressions *It's music to my ears* and *I'm all ears.* Search the Internet for three to five more idioms with the word *ear* or *ears.* Your teacher will tell you whether or not the idioms you find are common.

Key words: *idioms, ear, ears, body*

Proverb Web site These proverbs with the word *music* are from a Web site that lists proverbs from many countries. What do you think is the message in each proverb?

- The musician who is paid in advance does not play so well. — Spain
- If you've enjoyed the dance, pay the musicians. — Germany
- From a broken violin do not expect fine music. — Greece
- A silent mouth is musical. — Ireland
- Love begins with song and music and ends in a sea of tears. — Italy
- Those who can't dance say the music is no good. — Jamaica

Search the Internet for more proverbs with the words *music* or *musician.*

Speech Instructions—
Appendix C

B. Contact Assignment

In this lesson, you learned the expression *get out of a rut,* which includes the phrasal verb **get out of.** To learn more expressions with **get out (of),** with a partner ask a native speaker of English to help you fill out this chart. (For guidelines on how to do this kind of assignment, see Appendix F, "Contact Assignments," on page 197.)

Pronunciation Note: Remember to stress the second part of phrasal verbs.

	Meaning	**Sample Sentence**
get		
out (more often)	_____	_____
out of here out of doing something	_____	_____
something out of something	_____	_____
out of someone's hair	_____	_____

10. Expression Collection

Every week, find three expressions from the real world that are new to you. Keep an inventory in your notebook or on index cards, following the format in Appendix G, "Expression Collection," on page 198. Be ready to share what you found in small groups or with your entire class.

Collocation Match-Up

Collocations are special combinations of words. Collocations can be idioms or other phrases and expressions. Find collocations from *Lessons 7 and 8* by matching the words from Column A with the words in Column B. Sometimes more than one answer is possible. (You will probably be able to make additional expressions that are not from Lessons 7 and 8. Put these in the box.)

A		**B**
1. it hit	_____home_____	I know
2. get away	_____	on it
3. be wiped	_____	contention
4. drive someone	_____	money's worth
5. as far as	_____	no bearing on
6. in	_____	to write home about
7. sleep	_____	to be desired
8. get through	_____	home ✓
9. a bone of	_____	all ears
10. hop	_____	jet lag
11. I'm	_____	in
12. get my	_____	to someone
13. bring up	_____	with
14. leave a lot	_____	off
15. to top that	_____	depth
16. stretch	_____	up the wall
17. blow something	_____	a subject
18. nothing	_____	out of proportion
19. have	_____	out
20. get over	_____	out

Additional Collocations

Crossword Puzzle

Across

1   We all have our ups and ___.

5   She wants to get out of her ___, so she's looking for a new career.

6   She was so tired that she ___ keep her eyes open.

8   I'm sorry, but your argument just doesn't ___ water.

11   From his ___, everything is just fine.

12   Sorry, but that has no ___ on what we're talking about.

13   I can't decide now. I have to ___ on it and I'll tell you tomorrow.

16   When I heard the good news, I said it was ___ to my ears.

18   I need to ___ out for a few minutes. I'm really tired.

20   I ___ a bad case of jet lag, but I'm OK now.

Down

2   We've been talking for two hours, and we've hardly ___ the surface!

3   She got angry and blew everything out of ___.

4   Doesn't that noise drive you up the ___?

7   We had a great time and got ___ money's worth, that's for sure.

9   Tell me about it. I'm all ___.

10   They don't agree about that. It's a big ___ of contention between them.

11   He said he ___ on it and made his decision.

12   I wasn't very happy when you ___ up that subject again.

14   She thought the movie ___ a lot to be desired.

15   When the baby cried, it finally ___ home that they were parents.

17   I know you don't want me to ___ the subject, but we have to talk about it.

18   Maybe if I rest for a while, I'll get a ___ wind.

19   If you want a ride, ___ in.

Pronunciation

Part 1: Stress in Phrasal Verbs

Phrasal verbs are composed of verbs + words such as *in, on, at, up, down, out,* and *about*. Many of these small words are prepositions. Some phrasal verbs have three words.

In these exercises, you will learn to stress (emphasize) the *second* part of phrasal verbs. You will learn in Lesson 2 that we don't usually stress prepositions and other small words. In phrasal verbs, however, we make an exception—we stress these words.

Grammar Points to Remember About Phrasal Verbs

- When these expressions actually have three words (such as *put in for*), you cannot add words inside the expressions. They cannot be separated. They are "inseparable."
- When these expressions are in the passive voice (such as *be put off*), they cannot be separated.
- When phrasal verbs can be separated, they are called "separable." You can put words between them. For example,

He bottled up his feelings.	She put off her trip.
He bottled *his feelings* up.	She put *her trip* off.
He bottled *them* up.	She put *it* off.
Incorrect: ~~He bottled up them.~~	~~She put off it.~~

Notice, when used, a pronoun must come in the middle of the expression. It cannot come at the end.

Practice 1

Say these phrasal verbs from Lesson 1 aloud. Make the capitalized words stronger and louder than the other words.

3,I

bottled UP	pass AWAY
put OFF	pass BACK
hit it OFF	pass OUT
pass UP	put IN for
skip OVER	put someone UP

Practice 2

Listen to the sentences. Repeat what you hear. Then, with a partner, practice saying the sentences aloud.

1. I can't keep this *bottled UP* anymore. I'm tired of studying so hard!

2. I've always wanted to learn a lot of idioms, but I *put it OFF* for a long time because I was so busy studying grammar.

3. When I first heard the expression *hit it OFF*, I thought two people were hitting each other!

4. Now I have an opportunity to learn idioms. I don't want to *pass it UP*.

5. I used to *skip OVER* hard exercises, but I don't anymore.

6. My teacher told me that the expression *pass AWAY* is a euphemism. People don't like to say the word "die."

7. When she *passed BACK* the test, my heart was beating very fast.

8. I almost *passed OUT* when I saw that I got an 'A.'

9. When I *put IN for* a promotion at work and got it, I had to drop a class because I had to spend more time at work.

10. One of my classmates asked me too *put him UP* for a week because his apartment was being remodeled. That was good because we studied a lot together.

Part 2: Linking in Phrasal Verbs

To "link" means to connect. In English, we often link words when one word ends in a consonant sound and the next word starts with a vowel sound. The same happens when a word ends in a vowel sound and the next word starts with a consonant sound. This often occurs in phrasal verbs. (For more information on and practice with linking, see Lesson 5.)

Here are examples from Lesson 1:

Expression	Sounds like	
bottled‿up*	boddle-DUP*	/bɑdl-dʌ́p/
put‿it‿off	pu-di-DOFF*	/pə-dɪ-dɔ́f/
hit‿it‿off	hi-di-DOFF*	/hɪ-dɪ-dɔ́f/
pass‿up	pa-SUP	/pæ-sʌ́p/

*Notice that the *t*'s in these words sound like *d*'s. This situation occurs when:

- the *t* comes between vowel sounds as in *letter, what are,* etc.
- the *t* comes between a vowel and *l* as in *bottle.*

Practice 3

- Go back to the sentences in Practice 2 and insert linking lines between the words that should be linked in the phrasal verbs. For example, number 1 would be like this: bottled‿up.
- Practice saying these phrasal verbs aloud.
- Since the same pronunciation rule about linking vowel and consonant sounds applies to spoken English in general, you can also draw linking lines elsewhere in these sentences. For example, "I've‿always wanted to‿learn‿a‿lot‿of‿idioms." After you draw the lines, say the sentences aloud.

Practice 4: Put It All Together

- Locate the phrasal verbs in the introductory conversation and in the Exercise 1 mini-dialogues in Lessons 1. Circle the parts of phrasal verbs that should be stressed. Draw linking lines between the words that should be connected when spoken.
- Concentrate on stress and linking as you say the conversations with a partner.

Practice 5: Listen and Speak

3,3

Listen again to the introductory conversation in Lesson 1. Pay special attention to the pronunciation of phrasal verbs. If you can, record yourself and compare your pronunciation of phrasal verbs to the pronunciation on the audio program.

LESSON 2: Kids' Behavior in Public—The Bottom Line

Sentence Stress

In these exercises, you will learn which words are usually, but not always, stressed (emphasized) in phrases or sentences. Stressed words are the most important words in phrases and sentences because they carry the most information. Native speakers of English stress words that are the most important by making them stronger than the other words. They do this by making the stressed syllables in these words longer.

Practice 1*

To find out which words (nouns, verbs, prepositions, and other parts of speech) are usually (not always!) stressed or unstressed, look at the *Understanding the New Expressions* section and notice which words have stress marks. Then, on your own or with a partner, complete this chart by putting a check in the appropriate column. Some parts have been done for you.

	Usually stressed	Usually unstressed
Nouns	_____	_____
Pronouns	_____	_____
Possessive adjectives	_____	✓
Main verbs	_____	_____
Verb *be*	_____	_____
Phrasal verbs (1st part)	_____	_____
Phrasal verbs (2nd part)	_____	_____
Affirmative helping verbs	_____	✓
Negative helping verbs	✓	_____
Adjectives	_____	_____
Adverbs	✓	_____
Conjunctions	_____	✓
Prepositions	_____	_____
Articles	_____	_____
this/that/these/those	✓	_____
Wh question words	✓	_____

Practice 2

After you have completed the chart, go back to the *Understanding the New Expressions* section and say each expression aloud. Emphasize the stressed words.

The answers for this exercise can be found on page 220 in the Pronunciation Answer Key.

Practice 3

(A) With a partner, practice using the rules of sentence stress in this Mini-dialogue from Part 1 of Exercise 1 on page 13. The stressed words are underlined.

1. **A:** I <u>don't</u> <u>know</u> <u>where</u> <u>Laura</u> <u>is</u>.

   B: <u>Look</u>! <u>Here</u> she <u>comes</u>!

   (Forms of the verb be are stressed when they are the last word in a sentence.)

2. **A:** I <u>work</u> <u>40</u> <u>hours</u> a <u>week</u>, but I <u>hardly</u> <u>make</u> <u>any</u> <u>money</u>.

   B: <u>Well</u>, the <u>bottom</u> <u>line</u> is <u>that</u> you <u>need</u> to <u>get</u> <u>more</u> <u>education</u> so you can <u>get</u> a <u>better</u> <u>job</u>.

3. **A:** <u>How</u> did you <u>like</u> <u>that</u> <u>new</u> <u>restaurant</u>?

   B: I <u>liked</u> it, but my <u>friend</u> <u>didn't</u> <u>like</u> it at <u>all</u>.

4. **A:** You've <u>had</u> <u>nothing</u> at <u>all</u> to <u>eat</u>. Are you <u>OK</u>?

   B: I <u>think</u> <u>so</u>. I <u>just</u> <u>don't</u> <u>have</u> an <u>appetite</u> <u>right</u> <u>now</u>.

5. **A:** <u>Where</u> do they <u>live</u>?

   B: I <u>don't</u> <u>have</u> a <u>clue</u>.

6. **A:** I <u>couldn't</u> <u>believe</u> it! <u>All</u> of a <u>sudden</u>, he <u>started</u> <u>crying</u>.

   B: <u>So</u> <u>what</u> did you <u>do</u>?

(B) Look at Part 2 of Exercise 1 on page 13. Underline the stressed words. Then practice saying the mini-dialogues with a partner.*

Practice 4: Listen and Speak

(A) Listen to the recorded mini-dialogues in Exercise 1. Focus on sentence stress. Repeat what you hear.

3,4

(B) Underline the stressed words in the introductory dialogue on page 20. Then listen again to the recorded conversation. Repeat what you hear.

3,5

The answers for Practice 3B appear on page 220 in the Pronunciation Answer Key.

Intonation in Statements

You stress words that carry the most information, usually nouns, main verbs, adjectives, and adverbs. But one of these words will carry the most meaning in each phrase, clause, or sentence. That word, in addition to being stressed, should also be given the highest intonation (pitch). That word often contains *new* information for the listener.

Intonation, the rising and falling of your voice, helps you communicate meaning. High intonation communicates new information or what you think is most important, very high intonation communicates emotional feelings, and low intonation indicates that a sentence is ending. If you don't vary your intonation in English, you may give the impression that you are bored, and the people listening to you won't necessarily catch your meaning.

In the dialogue, Jan says, "This coffee is really strong."

- If she wants to emphasize *really*, she will say: This coffee is **really** strong.

- If she wants to emphasize *strong*, she will say: This coffee is really **strong**.*

THE MOST COMMON INTONATION PATTERN IN STATEMENTS

(A) Phrases, clauses, and sentences usually end with rising–falling intonation on the last stressed word. Notice that the lowest intonation comes at the end of a sentence. (And keep in mind that words are stressed by making their stressed syllables longer.)

1. If you want to know the ^{tru}th,* I was bored to ^{de}a_{th.}*

2. I have to stick it ^ou_{t.}*

3. One day it **dawned** on me that I was lucky to be in her ^{class} because I found myself ^{think}ing about what she said for days ^{af}ter.

*The words *strong, truth, death* and *out* have only one syllable, but notice how you can lengthen them and move from high to low intonation to indicate the end of a phrase or sentence.

(B) You can change this pattern if you want to emphasize a word containing new, important information. That word does not have to be the last stressed word in a phrase, clause, or sentence:

1. I ^{like} it that _{way.}

2. All during my last ^{class} I was thinking about ^{coming} here and could almost ^{taste} the cof_{fee.}

In sentence 1 above, *way* would usually be the last stressed word, but the speaker considers *like* more important. In sentence 2, the speaker wants to emphasize the new idea of *taste* more than the word *coffee*.

3,6

Practice 1

With a partner, say these sentences from the dialogue.

JAN: Mmm. This coffee is really str_ong.

STEVE: I ^{like} it that _{way.}

JAN: So do ^I_I. All during my last ^{class} I was thinking about ^{coming} here and could almost ^{taste} the cof_{fee.}

STEVE: Sounds like it wasn't too ^{exci}_{ting.}

3,7

Practice 2

Practice using rising-falling intonation with the underlined words. These are the last stressed words in the phrases, clauses, and sentences. Notice that these words come right before commas, dashes, and periods. Remember to pause when you see these punctuation marks. (You will learn the rules for "question intonation" in the next lesson.)

JAN: I was bored to <u>death</u>. I'm in that class only because it's a <u>requirement</u>, so I have to stick it <u>out</u>. The problem <u>is</u>, the professor doesn't know how to spark our <u>interest</u>. She just walks in and <u>lectures</u>. There's no <u>discussion</u>.

STEVE: What a <u>drag</u>! Don't people ask questions?

JAN: Oh, yeah, once in a blue <u>moon</u>. But I always see an awful lot of people <u>doodling</u>.

STEVE: I have only one big <u>lecture</u> class—world <u>history</u>—and the professor's the <u>best</u>. It's so <u>interesting</u>, I'm always on the edge of my <u>seat</u>. And when we have <u>discussions</u>, the room is filled with <u>electricity</u>.

Practice 3

Practice using rising intonation with the underlined words. These words are *not* the last stressed words of phrases, clauses, or sentences. Instead, they are important words that focus on new information.

3,8

1. I can tell their <u>minds</u> are wandering.

2. I'm jealous. Too bad I already <u>took</u> history.

3. I guess what it <u>really</u> comes down to is her <u>enthusiasm</u> for the subject. She just <u>loves</u> history. I started really <u>enjoying</u> school, especially <u>her</u> class.

4. You've got me really <u>curious</u> about this teacher.

Practice 4: Listen and Speak

As you refer to the pronunciation information and exercises, underline or circle the words that you think should receive the highest intonation in the introductory conversation. Then listen again to see if the speakers' voices go up and down as you expected. Notice how the words with the most information to communicate are stressed and given higher intonation. Also notice how rising-falling intonation indicates the end of a phrase, clause, or sentence. Say the conversation with a partner, and if you can, record yourselves and compare your intonation to that of the speakers.

3,9

Practice 5: Pronunciation—Review

Review the rules of sentence stress in Lesson 2. With a partner, say the mini-dialogues in Lesson 2, Practice 3 again. This time, however, add up arrows (↑) on the words that should receive the highest intonation. Add down arrows (↓) on the words that should receive the lowest intonation.

Intonation in Questions

Information (*Wh*) Questions

These end with rising-falling intonation. The stressed syllable of the last word that you want to stress should receive high intonation. After that, your voice will go down.

Information Questions (Rising-Falling Intonation)

1. What brings you to ^{this} neck of the woods?

2. About wh^at?

3. And guess wh^at?

4. How many hours do ^{YOU*} work a day?

Yes-No Questions

These questions end with rising intonation.

Yes-No Questions (Rising Intonation)

1. M^e?

2. Would you be willing to tell me your sto^{ry}?

3. You got about three ho^{urs}?

*While it is true that pronouns are usually not stressed, they are stressed to show a contrast. For example, I work eight hours a day. How many hours do YOU work?

In the conversation, the homeless man talks about how much he used to work and then asks the reporter, "How many hours do YOU work a day?" The emphasis on you shows the contrast between the two people.

Tag Questions

These questions start out with a statement and end with a short *yes-no* question. Use falling intonation if you are quite sure of the response you will receive, if you are expecting the listener to confirm what you have said. Use rising intonation if you are unsure.

Tag Questions

(Falling Intonation — You expect confirmation of what you've said.)

You think I grew up po͑or, don't you?

(Rising Intonation — You really don't know the answer.)

You think I grew up po͑or, don't you?

Practice 1

First, practice asking the preceding questions with a partner. Then, find the questions in the introductory conversation on pages 58 and 59 and write intonation arrows that show whether your voice should go up or down (↑↓).

Practice 2: Listen and Speak

Listen to the conversation again, and pay special attention to the intonation patterns used in questions. Perform the conversation with a partner, giving special attention to question intonation.

3,10

Practice 3

Choose a conversation from a lesson that you have already completed. Locate the questions and decide the kind of intonation they should receive. Write arrows that show whether your voice should go up or down. Then say the conversation with a partner.

Practice 4: Pronunciation—Review

Review the rules for intonation in statements on pages 156 and 157. Then apply these rules to Practice 3 above. Draw arrows on the words that should receive the highest intonation in both statements and questions. Practice reading Exercise 3 aloud.

Part 1: Thought Groups

Look at the following from the introductory conversation on page 76:

MICHAEL: (I'm in shock,) (to say the least.) (This is really all beyond my comprehension.) (It hasn't sunk in yet . . .) (maybe it never will.)

JENNIE: (Well,) (I've got to hand it to you.) (You sure look very calm.) (If I were in your shoes,) (I don't think I'd be able to stand still,) (let alone buy presents for people) (and have conversations with them.)

Notice the groups of words in parentheses. Each group expresses a thought and is called a *thought group*. By saying each group of words without pausing between the words, we create a certain rhythm.

At the end of each thought group, our voices go down in pitch and we sometimes pause briefly.

If you say each word equally with pauses between them, you won't be using English rhythm. This can make your English difficult to understand, even if you are using clear pronunciation of sounds and correct grammar and vocabulary.

Question: How can you know what words make up a thought group?

Answer: What goes into a thought group can vary, so it's not possible to give rules for 100 percent of the time. But you can follow these general guidelines:

What may be a thought group	Example
• a short sentence	*(I've got to hand it to you.)*
• a phrase	*(to say the least)*
• a clause	*(If I were you,)*
• transition words	*you know, well, first, next, finally*

In writing, commas, periods, and other punctuation marks indicate the ends of thought groups. These markers help make written language more understandable. In speech, changes in pitch and short pauses make our spoken language more understandable to our listeners.

Practice 1

Put parentheses around the thought groups in the introductory conversation on page 76. Don't be afraid to guess. Say the words in the thought groups to yourself to see if they feel naturally grouped.

Example:
You don't say: (What's) (gotten) (into) (Michael?)   (What's) (he) (doing?)
You say: (What's gotten into Michael?)   (What's he doing?)

Part 2: Linking

As you know from Lesson 1, linking means connecting. In English, we often link words within thought groups, and that may be one reason why you may not always understand what you hear, but are able to understand the same words when they are written.

The following are some of the situations in which we link words:

1.   when a word ends in a consonant *sound* and the next word starts with a vowel *sound.* ("Come" ends in the letter 'e,' but the consonant sound 'm.')

    A.   Come‿on.   That's‿unheard‿of.
          | | | | | |
       /m/ /a/   /s/ /ə/   /d/ /ʌ/

    B.   The 'h' sound in *he, his, her,* and *him* is often dropped when these words are not the first word in a sentence. As a result, these words are often linked to words that precede them.

Full word	Shortened word	Example
he	'e	What's‿'e doing?
his	'is	Where's‿'is car?
her	'er	Where's‿'er car?
him	'im	Tell‿'im 'Congratulations!'

2. When the final consonant sound of one word is the same as the beginning sound of the next word. (Say this sound only once.)

Two Words

It was the firs**t t**ime I ever bought a lottery ticket. I've	firs-time
go**t t**o hand it to you.	go-da*
. . . let alone buy presents for people and have conversations wi**th th**em.	wi-them
Right now my who**le l**ife's up in the air. You'**re r**ight not to make any quick decisions.	ho-life's
	yo-right
Be on the lookout for people who wan**t t**o take advantage of you.	wanta *or* wanna

Sounds vs. Spelling

Be careful not to confuse letters from the alphabet and actual sounds. When you are linking words, look at and listen for the sounds rather than the letters.

Look at the word *university.* It starts with the vowel letter *u,* but the first sound in this word is really /y/. Also look at the word *hour.* It starts with the consonant letter *h,* but the first sound in this word is really the vowel /au/. And don't let words that end in silent vowels fool you. The last letter in the word *come* is *e,* but the last sound is really /m/.

See note about t's and d's at the bottom of page 152.

Practice 2

Go back to the introductory conversation and insert linking lines between the words within the thought groups. Practice saying the thought groups aloud again, but this time also focus on linking.

Practice 3: Listen and Speak

Listen again to the introductory conversation. Pay special attention to how the speakers create thought groups. Notice that they don't say words individually. Also listen for words that are linked together. If you can, record yourself and compare your pronunciation to the pronunciation on the audio program.

3,11

Practice 4: Pronunciation—Review

Review the rules for stress and linking in phrasal verbs in Lesson 1. Then, in any of the conversations in Lessons 2, 3, 4, or 5, apply these rules to the phrasal verbs that you have learned. Circle the words that should receive the most stress, and draw linking lines where necessary.

Part 1: Contractions

Pronounce the following contractions from the "Stuck in the Elevator" conversation. (When a contraction has more than one syllable, the stressed syllable is in capital letters.)

Contractions	Pronunciation	
can't	kant	/kænt/
what's	wuts	/wʌts/
I'm	eyem	/aɪm/
wasn't	WUzint	/wʌ́-zɪnt/
don't	dont	/doʊnt/
they'll	thayl	/ðeɪl/
isn't	iznt	/í-zɪnt/
we'll	weeel	/wil/
you're	yor	/yɔr/
I'd	eyed	/aɪd/
Let's	lets	/lɛts/
you've	yoov	/yuv/
that'll	THAdul	/ðǽ-dəl/

Practice 1: Speak

Underline the contractions in the conversation and then practice saying the conversation with a partner.

Part 2: Reduced Forms (Reductions)

As you know, many words that you have difficulty understanding in fast speech are easily recognizable to you when they are written in their full forms. The reason for your difficulty in understanding is that native speakers often "reduce" the full forms when they speak. Take a look at this list of the full and reduced forms that appear in this lesson's introductory conversation. (When a reduced form has more than one syllable, the stressed syllable is in capital letters.)

3,13

Full form	Pronunciation of reduced form	
out of	OWda	/aʊ́də/
going to	GONna or GOing ta	/gʌ́nə/ /góʊɪŋtə/
to	ta	/tə/
would have been	WUDuv been	/wʌ́dəvbɪn/
do you	da ya	/dəyə/
don't know	doNO or duNO	/doʊnóʊ/
for	fer	/fər/
you	ya	/yə/
Have to	HAFta	/hǽftə/
and	'n	/ən/
you're	yer	/yər/
or	er	/ər/
Climbing	CLI-min´	/kláɪmɪn/
don't you	DONcha	/dóʊntʃə/

Practice 2: Listen

Circle the full forms listed above in the introductory conversation. Then listen to the audio program to see if you can hear how their reduced forms are pronounced. You do not need to be concerned about actually saying the reduced forms, but recognizing them when you hear them will help your comprehension.

3,14

Practice 3: Pronunciation—Review

Review the rules for stress and intonation in Lessons 1 through 4. Then apply these rules to the conversation of the three people in Exercise 4 of this lesson on page 160. Circle or put accent marks on the words that should receive the most stress, and draw arrows to indicate where the intonation should go up or down. Then, in groups of three, say the Exercise 3 conversation aloud.

LESSON 7: Violence in the Media— A Bone of Contention

3,15

Voiced and Voiceless Consonants and the *-ed* Ending

The final *ed* that is used to form the past tense of regular verbs can have three sounds: the voiceless /t/, the voiced /d/, or a new syllable/ɪd/. To determine which sound to use, you need to know whether the last sound (not letter) of a word is voiced or voiceless. All vowel sounds are voiced.

You can feel whether consonant sounds are voiced or voiceless by holding your hand against your throat and saying the sounds. If you feel a vibration, the sound is voiced.

Don't feel that it is necessary to memorize the chart below. It is for your reference. The best strategy for you when working on your pronunciation is to listen very carefully to the speech of native speakers.

CONSONANTS

Letters	Sounds	Voiced	Voiceless	Example
b	/b/	x		**b**ut
c	/k/		x	**c**omputer
	/s/		x	**s**cience
d	/d/	x		**d**inosaur
f	/f/		x	**f**orget
g	/g/	x		for**g**et
	/dʒ/	x		technolo**g**y
h	/h/		x	**h**ome
j	/dʒ/	x		**j**udge
k	/k/		x	thin**k**
l	/l/	x		mai**l**
m	/m/	x		progra**m**
n	/n/	x		wo**n**
p	/p/		x	com**p**uter
q	/kw/		x	**q**uite
r	/r/	x		**r**eally
s	/s/		x	u**s**
	/z/	x		i**s**
	/ʒ/	x		u**s**ual
t	/t/		x	grea**t**
v	/v/	x		**v**ery
w	/w/	x		**w**on
x	/ks/		x	si**x**
y	/y/	x		**y**ou
z	/z/	x		**z**oo
ch	/tʃ/		x	**ch**ange
	/ʃ/		x	ma**ch**ine
	/k/		x	te**ch**nology
sh	/ʃ/		x	**sh**e
th	/ð/	x		**th**is
	/θ/		x	**th**ink
ng	/ŋ/	x		thi**ng**

-ed Past Tense Ending Rules

Final sound of regular verb	Pronunciation of *-ed* ending	New syllable added?	Example
voiceless	/t/	no	*loo**k**ed* = /lʊk**t**/
voiced	/d/	no	*cau**s**ed* = /kɔz**d**/
/t/ or /d/	/ɪd/	yes	*wan**t**ed* = /wɑnt**ɪd**/
			*nee**d**ed* = /nídɪd/

3,16

Practice 1*

Look at the list of some of the regular verbs from this lesson's introductory conversation.

- Say the base form of each verb. Write the final sound of each of these verbs on the lines.
- If the final sound is /t/ or /d/, then circle the /ɪd/ past tense ending in the column on the right.
- For all the other base forms of verbs, decide if the final sound is voiced or voiceless. (Remember that all vowel sounds are voiced. For consonant sounds, look at the chart on page 169.)
- Circle whether the past tense forms of these verbs should end in the voiceless /t/ or voiced /d/ sound.
- With a partner, say both the base form and past tense form of each verb.

Base form of verb	Final sound	Past tense	Final -ed sound
1. like	_k_	liked	/t̸/ /d/ /ɪd/
2. show	____	showed	/t/ /d/ /ɪd/
3. end	____	ended	/t/ /d/ /ɪd/
4. look	____	looked	/t/ /d/ /ɪd/
5. listen	____	listened	/t/ /d/ /ɪd/
6. want	____	wanted	/t/ /d/ /ɪd/
7. hope	____	hoped	/t/ /d/ /ɪd/
8. agree	____	agreed	/t/ /d/ /ɪd/
9. start	____	started	/t/ /d/ /ɪd/
10. disagree	____	disagreed	/t/ /d/ /ɪd/

The answers to Practice 1 appear on page 221 in the Pronunciation Answer Key.

Practice 2*

- Read the following paragraphs silently. As you read, write above the underlined words how to pronounce the *-ed* endings: /t/, /d/, or /ɪd/.
- Look at the words that follow the *-ed* sounds. If any of these words start with a vowel sound, write linking lines between the *-ed* and the vowel sound that follows. (See Lesson 5 on linking.)
- After you have finished marking these paragraphs, listen to how they sound on the audio program.
- Take turns reading the paragraphs aloud with a partner.

3,17

/t/
Two people went to a violent movie. One of them <u>liked</u> it a lot, and the

other <u>hated</u> it. The movie <u>showed</u> a lot of blood and killing, and it <u>ended</u> with

probably a hundred people dead. Of course, the person who <u>disliked</u> the movie

<u>wanted</u> to leave as soon as it <u>started</u>, but she <u>agreed</u> to stay because her friend

<u>wanted</u> to stay.

After the movie, they <u>talked</u> for a while. The woman <u>claimed</u> that

violence in the media <u>affected</u> the way children <u>behaved</u>, and gave them

examples of how people <u>committed</u> crimes. Her friend <u>listened</u> and said he

<u>hoped</u> she was wrong.

The answers to Practice 2 appear on page 221 in the Pronunciation Answer Key.

Practice 3

- In the introductory conversations of any other lessons that you have studied, look for ten regular verbs.
- Put the past tense forms of these verbs in the chart below.
- Circle the pronunciation of the *-ed* endings and write in the word that follows each verb. Decide whether or not these words should be linked.
- After you have completed the chart, practice saying the past tense verbs and the words that come after them. Link these words when necessary.

Past tense verbs	Pronunciation of *-ed* ending			Word that follows	Linked?		From Lesson
1. _____	/t/	/d/	/ɪd/	_____	Yes	No	_____
2. _____	/t/	/d/	/ɪd/	_____	Yes	No	_____
3. _____	/t/	/d/	/ɪd/	_____	Yes	No	_____
4. _____	/t/	/d/	/ɪd/	_____	Yes	No	_____
5. _____	/t/	/d/	/ɪd/	_____	Yes	No	_____
6. _____	/t/	/d/	/ɪd/	_____	Yes	No	_____
7. _____	/t/	/d/	/ɪd/	_____	Yes	No	_____
8. _____	/t/	/d/	/ɪd/	_____	Yes	No	_____
9. _____	/t/	/d/	/ɪd/	_____	Yes	No	_____
10. _____	/t/	/d/	/ɪd/	_____	Yes	No	_____

Practice 4: Listen and Speak

The dictations in Appendix A, starting on page 178, are all in the past tense. Choose a dictation from a lesson that you have already studied, and circle regular past tense verbs. Then, near each of these verbs, mark which of the three *-ed* endings you think you should use: /t/, /d/, or /ɪd/.

3,18

Listen to the dictation to check, and then practice saying the past tense verbs aloud. When you are ready, dictate the paragraph or paragraphs to a partner or small group.

Practice 5: Pronunciation—Review

As you read this lesson's introductory conversation on pages 114 to 115, listen again to the audio program. See if you can spot any reduced forms (see Lesson 6). There is no need to repeat the reduced forms, but there is a need for you to learn to recognize them as they are spoken by native speakers.

3,19

LESSON 8: Changing Time Zones—A Bad Case of Jet Lag

Voiced and Voiceless Consonants and the *-s* Ending

The final *s* is used to indicate:

- the third person singular form of verbs (sleep**s**)
- possessives (Dad'**s**)
- regular noun plurals (classe**s**)

These *s* endings can have three sounds: the voiceless /s/, the voiced /z/, or a new syllable, /ɪz/.

To determine which sound to use, you need to know whether the last sound (not letter) of a word is voiced or voiceless. All vowels are voiced.

To find out whether particular consonant sounds are voiced or voiceless, look at the consonant chart on page 169.

	Final -s Ending Rules		
Final sound of word	**Pronunciation of -s ending**	**New syllable added?**	**Examples**
voiceless	/s/	no	*sleeps* = /slip**s**/
voiced	/z/	no	*Dad's* = /dæd**z**/
s, z, sh, ch, j, x	/ɪz/	yes	*classes* = /klæs-**ɪz**/

Practice 1*

Look at the list of some of the regular nouns from this lesson's introductory conversation.

- Say the singular form of each noun. Write the final sound of each noun on the lines.
- If the final sound is *s, z, sh, ch, j,* or *x,* then circle the /ɪz/ final sound in the column on the right.
- For all the other singular nouns, decide if the final sound is voiced or voiceless. (Remember that all vowels are voiced. For consonant sounds, look at the chart on page 169.)
- Circle whether the plural forms of these nouns should end in the voiceless /s/ or voiced /z/ sound.
- With a partner, say both the singular and plural form of each noun.

3,20

Singular noun	Final sound	Plural noun	Final -s sound		
1. trip	_p_	trips	(/s/)	/z/	/ɪz/
2. afternoon	___	afternoons	/s/	/z/	/ɪz/
3. walk	___	walks	/s/	/z/	/ɪz/
4. eye	___	eyes	/s/	/z/	/ɪz/
5. night	___	nights	/s/	/z/	/ɪz/
6. country	___	countries	/s/	/z/	/ɪz/
7. surface	___	surfaces	/s/	/z/	/ɪz/
8. winter	___	winters	/s/	/z/	/ɪz/
9. holiday	___	holidays	/s/	/z/	/ɪz/
10. roommate	___	roommates	/s/	/z/	/ɪz/
11. class	___	classes	/s/	/z/	/ɪz/
12. chance	___	chances	/s/	/z/	/ɪz/

The answers to Practice 1 appear on page 222 in the Pronunciation Answer Key.

Practice 2*

Look at some of the verbs from this lesson's introductory conversation.

- Say the base form of each verb. Write the final sound of each verb on the lines.
- If the final sound is *s, z, sh, ch, j,* or *x,* then circle the /ɪz/ final sound in the column on the right.
- For all the other base forms of verbs, decide if the final sound is voiced or voiceless. (Remember that all vowels are voiced. For consonant sounds, look at the chart on page 169.)
- Circle whether the third person singular forms of these verbs should end in the voiceless /s/ or voiced /z/ sound.
- With a partner, say both the base form and third person singular form of each verb.

Base form of verb	Final sound	Third person singular form	Final -*s* sound		
1. know	o	knows	/s/	/z/	(/ɪz/)
2. sleep	___	sleeps	/s/	/z/	/ɪz/
3. take	___	takes	/s/	/z/	/ɪz/
4. tell	___	tells	/s/	/z/	/ɪz/
5. stretch	___	stretches	/s/	/z/	/ɪz/
6. miss	___	misses	/s/	/z/	/ɪz/
7. think	___	thinks	/s/	/z/	/ɪz/
8. help	___	helps	/s/	/z/	/ɪz/
9. live	___	lives	/s/	/z/	/ɪz/
10. realize	___	realizes	/s/	/z/	/ɪz/
11. improve	___	improves	/s/	/z/	/ɪz/
12. lose	___	loses	/s/	/z/	/ɪz/

3.21

The answers to Practice 2 appear on page 222 in the Pronunciation Answer Key.

Practice 3*

- Read the following paragraphs silently. As you read, write above the underlined words how to pronounce the -s endings—as /s/, /z/, or /ɪz/.
- Look at the words that follow the -s sounds. If any of these words start with a vowel sound, write linking lines between the -s and the vowel sound that follows. (See Lesson 5 on linking.)
- After you have finished marking these paragraphs, listen to how they sound on the audio program.
- Take turns reading the paragraphs aloud with a partner.

3.22

/s/

Kate's asleep, and her mother, Julia, <u>tries</u> to wake her up and get her to come to dinner. Kate <u>asks</u> her mother to let her sleep, but her mother <u>knows</u> that she <u>needs</u> to get up. Julia <u>decides</u> that Kate will get up if she <u>keeps</u> talking to her. First, she <u>asks</u> Kate about her <u>plans</u> and <u>tells</u> her that she <u>hopes</u> she'll stay home next year. Then she <u>suggests</u> that Kate tell her about her <u>friends</u>, but Kate <u>says</u> that she's too tired to talk.

When Kate <u>asks</u> her mother to talk about how she has been, Julia <u>confesses</u> that she has had her <u>ups</u> and <u>downs</u>. She <u>explains</u> that with all her <u>kids</u> gone, the house has been very quiet. Then, when Julia <u>notices</u> that Kate is starting to fall asleep again, she <u>pulls</u> the blanket off and Julia <u>laughs</u>. Finally, she <u>gets</u> up and <u>says</u>, "You won, Mom. What's for dinner?"

The answers to Practice 3 appear on page 222 in the Pronunciation Answer Key.

Practice 4

- In the introductory conversations of any other lessons that you have studied, look for five plural nouns and five third person singular verbs.
- Put the -s forms of these words in the chart below.
- Circle the pronunciation of the -s endings. Then write the word that follows each plural noun or third person singular verb. Decide whether or not these words should be linked.
- After you have completed the chart, practice saying the plural nouns and third person singular verbs + the words that come after them. Link these words when necessary.

-s ending word	Pronunciation of -s ending	Word that follows	Linked?	From Lesson
1. _____	/s/ /z/ /ɪz/	_____	Yes No	_____
2. _____	/s/ /z/ /ɪz/	_____	Yes No	_____
3. _____	/s/ /z/ /ɪz/	_____	Yes No	_____
4. _____	/s/ /z/ /ɪz/	_____	Yes No	_____
5. _____	/s/ /z/ /ɪz/	_____	Yes No	_____
6. _____	/s/ /z/ /ɪz/	_____	Yes No	_____
7. _____	/s/ /z/ /ɪz/	_____	Yes No	_____
8. _____	/s/ /z/ /ɪz/	_____	Yes No	_____
9. _____	/s/ /z/ /ɪz/	_____	Yes No	_____
10. _____	/s/ /z/ /ɪz/	_____	Yes No	_____

Practice 5: Listen and Speak

Listen again to the introductory conversation on pages 130 and 131, paying special attention to the pronunciation of the -s endings. If possible, record yourself saying the conversation, and then analyze your pronunciation of these endings.

3,23

Practice 6: Pronunciation—Review

Review the information about thought groups and linking in Lesson 5. Then listen to the conversation in Exercise 4 on pages 142 and 143, and insert parentheses and linking lines where you think they belong. With a partner, say the conversation.

Appendices

Appendix A

Dictations (Exercise 6)

Lesson 1, Page 16

Two guys, Al and Bill, were at a party. Al noticed that something was bothering Bill, so he asked him what was eating him. At first, Bill didn't want to say anything, but then he admitted that there was a woman he wanted to talk to, but he didn't have the guts to start a conversation. He said the woman wouldn't want to be caught dead with him, but Al kept telling him to take the initiative and walk over to her. Finally Bill realized that if he passed up this chance, he'd never forgive himself.

Lesson 2, Page 33

One evening at a restaurant, a man and woman were shocked by a child's behavior. The little boy was out of control, running around, while his parents didn't have a clue that he was causing trouble. They were just enjoying their dinner.

The other couple was upset because they had gone through the trouble of getting a babysitter for their own kids. They just wanted an evening out so they could relax and have dinner in peace. They were also upset because the restaurant was noisy and it was taking forever to get their food.

They told the waitress that the bottom line was that parents had to keep their kids under control and teach them how to behave in public.

Lesson 3, Page 54

After class, Jan and Steve were talking at a cafe. Jan was telling him how bored to death she was in one of her classes. She explained that she would stick it out because the class was required, but complained that the professor didn't know how to spark students' interest.

Steve listened to her, and then told her about an exciting history class that he was taking. It was so exciting, in fact, that he was always on the edge of his seat.

He admitted that at the beginning of the semester he had been fooling around a lot and even bombed a test. But he finally buckled down and worked hard, and found that he was really enjoying his class.

Lesson 4, Page 70

In an interview with a reporter, a homeless man revealed a great deal about his past. He admitted that if his parents knew that he was living on the streets, they would roll over in their graves.

The reporter was surprised to learn that the man had a college degree, and that he had once worked for a big company. Although he had some trouble keeping up with all the work that they gave him, he kept moving up the ladder. The problem was, however, that he was getting burned out and had no time for his family. Eventually his wife left him, and then the company he had worked so hard for closed down.

Lesson 5, Page 90

Michael, who just won ten million dollars in the lottery, went to his office to give out gifts to his friends. He told everyone that winning all that money was beyond his comprehension and that it really hadn't sunk in yet. He also said that he had no idea what was in store for him, but he was going to make sure that the money wouldn't go down the drain.

When someone asked if he was going to quit his job, he said he didn't know yet, but that he wouldn't rule it out. His friends advised him to be on the lookout for people who wanted to take advantage of him, and he promised them that he would be very careful.

Lesson 6, Page 107

Mr. Claustrophobia (Mr. C.) and Mrs. Calm were surprised to find themselves stuck in an elevator. While Mr. C. complained a lot and showed that he was afraid, Mrs. Calm tried to calm him down.

In fact, when Mr. C. told her that he was at the end of his rope and that he didn't know what he would do if he was going to be cooped up in the elevator for a long time, Mrs. Calm told him not to lose his head. She told him that they would have to make do until help arrived, and that they were lucky to have both light and company. To avoid dwelling on the scary situation they were in, Mrs. Calm encouraged Mr. C. to tell her his life story.

Lesson 7, Page 125

Angela and Jason went to a movie. Angela felt that it was nothing to write home about, while Jason loved it. Angela said it had too much violence and that the violence had no bearing on the story. But Jason said he felt that the violent scenes were important parts of the story.

When Angela told Jason that his argument didn't hold water, he accused her of blowing the whole thing out of proportion. Finally, they agreed to disagree and decided to get a cup of coffee. After all, they really love each other, even though they sometimes drive each other crazy.

Lesson 8, Page 144

A daughter who had been studying in another country for a year just returned home and had a conversation with her father. The problem was, she just wanted to go to bed because she had jet lag. Wanting to keep her awake because it was the middle of the afternoon, her father suggested that they take a walk. He thought that she might get a second wind from taking a walk and getting some fresh air.

On the walk, they talked about how they had missed each other. The daughter described her ups and downs while she was away, and explained that holidays were the hardest times for her. She had been homesick a lot. But when spring came, she said it hit home that she was very lucky to have the opportunity to study abroad, and she started to get out of her rut. She ended up having a great time.

Walk and Talk Forms (Exercise 7)

Directions
- Put the names of the students you talk to in the spaces on the left.
- Ask each person no more than two questions. Then move on to someone else.
- Don't ask the same question more than once.
- Write very short notes in the spaces after each question. Don't write full sentences. Write just enough so you remember what your partners said. As you write, try to frequently look up at the person you are talking to.
- After you have completed this activity, write what your classmates said on a separate sheet of paper. As you write, be sure to include the new expressions in your sentences. To check what you have written, you can *Walk and Talk* again and show your writing to the students you interviewed.

Walk and Talk—Lesson 1, page 17

_____ 1. Are you the kind of person who keeps things that bother you bottled up inside, or do you get things off your chest? Explain, and give some examples.

_____ 2. What are two activities or sports that scare you? Why don't you have the guts to do those things?

_____ 3. Do you generally do things on time, or do you put things off? Explain by giving some examples.

_____ 4. Have you ever hit it off with anyone immediately? Explain the circumstances.

_____ 5. What do you think life is bound to be like in fifty years?

_____ 6. What is one kind of food that you can never pass up?

_____ 7. What are two ways students can take the initiative to speak to native speakers of English?

Walk and Talk—Lesson 2, pages 33–34

_____ 1. In your native culture, is it common for parents to take children to restaurants? How common is it to get a babysitter?

_____ 2. In your native culture, how do parents punish their children?

_____ 3. When you are disturbed by noise at a restaurant or movie theater, what do you do? (a) Nothing? (b) Talk directly to the people who are bothering you? (c) Talk to the manager? Explain.

_____ 4. What do you do when someone near you at a restaurant or movie theater is talking on a cell phone? Do you have your cell phone on when you're in restaurants or theaters? If yes, do you think about how loud you are talking?

_____ 5. What can't you put up with in the following places? (a) at school (b) at home (c) in a store (d) in a restaurant (e) in a theater (f) in a bus (g) train or plane

_____ 6. What is one part of the world that you don't have a clue about?

_____ 7. What are some places where you can read, relax, or study in peace?

_____ 8. Do you think it will take forever to learn enough English? Why or why not?

Walk and Talk—Lesson 3, page 54

_____ 1. What are two or three things that bore you to death?

_____ 2. Think of a situation that you couldn't stand being in (perhaps a party, a wedding, a trip, a show). Did you stick it out to the end? Why or why not?

_____ 3. Which subjects that you have studied in school sparked your interest? Which didn't spark your interest?

_____ 4. Were you ever a lazy student? If yes, did you eventually buckle down and become more serious about doing your work? Explain.

_____ 5. What kind of food do you like an awful lot? What kind of people do you like an awful lot? Why?

_____ 6. In what situations do you often find your mind wandering?

_____ 7. Everyone has had the experience of being on the edge of their seat at some kind of show, movie, or other type of performance. Describe one experience that you have had.

Walk and Talk—Lesson 4, page 70

_____ 1. Is there a minimum wage in your native country? Is it enough for people to live on?

_____ 2. Is it common for people you know to live from paycheck to paycheck, or do they actually save money?

_____ 3. What does a person need to do to move up the ladder in your native country? Are the opportunities to move up the same for men and women? Explain.

_____ 4. Do you know anyone who has worked too much day in and day out and then gotten burned out? If yes, explain the situation.

_____ 5. What do you think are some steps that need to be taken to end homelessness?

Walk and Talk—Lesson 5, page 90

_____ I. Do you have an expression similar to "beginner's luck" in your native language? If yes, what is it? What are some symbols of good luck and bad luck in your native culture?

_____ 2. If you won millions of dollars in a lottery, what would you do with the money?

_____ 3. What is Michael's mother (in Exercise 4) worried about? Read her e-mail again, and make a list of her concerns about his sudden wealth. Add any concerns that you might have.

_____ 4. What are some American customs that are unheard of in your native country? What are some customs in your native country that are unheard of in the United States?

_____ 5. What aspects of your life are up in the air?

_____ 6. Describe a time when your efforts to do something went down the drain.

_____ 7. Describe the life of someone (real or imaginary) who's got it made.

_____ 1. People from different cultural backgrounds may behave differently with strangers in places such as elevators. Some factors include the physical distance between them and whether or not they make eye contact or talk. In your native culture, how far do people usually stand from each other in crowded and uncrowded elevators? Do they make eye contact with each other? What do they look at? Do they talk to each other?

_____ 2. What are three to five events that can happen out of the blue and surprise people? Make a list.

_____ 3. Are people in your native country generally better off or worse off financially than they were twenty or thirty years ago? Explain.

_____ 4. When people don't have enough money to buy a lot of things, what are some things they do to "make do"?

_____ 5. What are some kinds of work that you have knocked yourself out doing?

Walk and Talk—Lesson 7, pages 125–126

_____ 1. Think about when you were a child. Do you remember any particular instance when something you saw in the movies or on TV really scared you? Do you think having experiences like this is good or bad for children?

_____ 2. Have you heard of any problems that have come up when children have gone on the Internet and participated in chat room discussions? How do you think parents and others can protect children from dangers on the Internet?

_____ 3. When you were a child did your parents let you get away with murder, or were they strict? Explain.

_____ 4. From your standpoint, how should parents discipline their children—with words or by striking them physically?

_____ 5. The news media are often accused of blowing stories out of proportion. In other words, they may take a story and make it sound more important than it really is. What do you think? (If possible, give examples from the news.)

_____ 6. Give an example of a bone of contention between you and someone you know. Or, if you'd rather not get too personal, give an example of a bone of contention between two people that you know.

Walk and Talk—Lesson 8, pages 144–145

_____ 1. Do you think young people should live with their parents until they get married? Or, do you think it's good for young people to move out of their parents' home at around 18 and learn to be independent? Explain.

_____ 2. Have you ever had jet lag? If yes, where were you? What did you do to stay awake? If you were awake when everyone else was sleeping, what did you do?

_____ 3. If you are living in a foreign culture, or if you have ever lived in a foreign culture, describe some of the ups and downs that you have experienced.

_____ 4. What are one or two subjects that you'd like to learn about in depth? Be specific and explain why a subject interests you. (Possible subjects: history, politics, psychology, education, care of children, care of the elderly, space research, the environment, linguistics.)

_____ 5. Have you or someone you know ever been in a rut (e.g., unhappy in a job/depressed because of a boring routine)? If yes, what was the problem? Talk about ways to get out of a rut.

Speech Instructions—Exercise 9A

Research a speech topic suggested in Exercise 9A. As you do your research, narrow your topic to a specific area that you want to focus on. Your teacher will give you a time limit for your speech.

Questions you might ask:

1. What are some tips on making a good speech?
   Have a clear outline (see page 189), use a visual aid if possible, and have good eye contact with your audience. The twelve items listed on the speech evaluation forms (see page 90) include the characteristics of a good speech.

2. How should I practice?
   • Find a quiet place.
   • Practice the speech out loud more than once. Time your speech.
   • Record your speech if you can.

3. Can I read my speech?
   No. You will need to put short notes (not sentences) on note cards. (But you can write the first and last sentence on a card.) If you use more than one note card, number your cards.

4. Can I memorize my speech?
   No. If you memorize your speech, it will sound like you are reading it. It is better to just look quickly at notes and then make your own sentences.

5. How should I start and end my speech?
   Possible techniques for starting: tell a story (an anecdote), give background information, use a quotation. Then say "Today I'm going to talk about ___."

   Possible techniques for ending: give a short summary, evaluate the significance of what you have said/give your opinion, use a quotation, make a prediction. Then say "Thank you. Are there any questions?" (Don't end with "That's all.")

Sample Note Card

Introduction: story about how my parents met

Introductory Sentence: Today I'm going to talk about dating customs in three different countries.

· in the U.S.

  ·

  ·

· in my native country

  ·

  ·

· in _____

  ·

  ·

Conclusion: My opinion about dating customs

Concluding Sentence: Thank you. Are there any questions?

Speech Evaluation Forms

SPEECH EVALUATION BY TEACHER

Name of Speaker: _____ **Grade:** _____

		Disagree Strongly				Agree Strongly
1.	The main idea was clearly stated.	1	2	3	4	5
2.	Enough details were given to clarify the main idea.	1	2	3	4	5
3.	The speech was well organized.	1	2	3	4	5
4.	The speech was well prepared.	1	2	3	4	5

The speaker:

5.	showed interest in the topic.	1	2	3	4	5
6.	glanced at brief notes and didn't read a written speech.	1	2	3	4	5
7.	spoke clearly, at a moderate speed.	1	2	3	4	5
8.	spoke in a voice that was neither too loud nor too soft.	1	2	3	4	5
9.	recognized when it was necessary to define words and/or give an example.	1	2	3	4	5
10.	used visual aids as necessary.	1	2	3	4	5
11.	used eye contact effectively—that is, looked at people in all parts of the room.	1	2	3	4	5
12.	used humor and smiled when appropriate.	1	2	3	4	5

Pronunciation Notes   **Grammar/Vocabulary Notes**

_____   _____

_____   _____

Comments

_____

_____

_____

SPEECH EVALUATION BY CLASSMATE

Name of Speaker: _____ **Name of Peer Evaluator:** _____

NOTE: Each speech should have at least two peer evaluators.

	Disagree Strongly				Agree Strongly
1. The main idea was clearly stated	1	2	3	4	5
2. Enough details were given to clarify the main idea.	1	2	3	4	5
3. The speech was well organized.	1	2	3	4	5
4. The speech was well prepared.	1	2	3	4	5

The speaker:

	Disagree Strongly				Agree Strongly
5. showed interest in the topic.	1	2	3	4	5
6. glanced at brief notes and didn't read a written speech.	1	2	3	4	5
7. spoke clearly, at a moderate speed.	1	2	3	4	5
8. spoke in a voice that was neither too loud nor too soft.	1	2	3	4	5
9. recognized when it was necessary to define words and/or give an example.	1	2	3	4	5
10. used visual aids as necessary.	1	2	3	4	5
11. used eye contact effectively—that is, looked at people in all parts of the room.	1	2	3	4	5
12. used humor and smiled when appropriate.	1	2	3	4	5

I recommend that next time you _____

_____

_____

One thing very good about your speech was _____

_____

_____

SPEECH SELF-EVALUATION

Name: _____

NOTE: Do this evaluation after watching the videotape of your speech, if possible.

		Disagree Strongly				Agree Strongly
1.	The main idea was clearly stated.	1	2	3	4	5
2.	I gave enough details to clarify the main idea.	1	2	3	4	5
3.	My speech was well organized.	1	2	3	4	5
4.	My speech was well prepared.	1	2	3	4	5
5.	I showed interest in the topic.	1	2	3	4	5
6.	I glanced at brief notes and didn't read a written speech.	1	2	3	4	5
7.	I spoke clearly, at a moderate speed.	1	2	3	4	5
8.	I spoke in a voice that was neither too loud nor too soft.	1	2	3	4	5
9.	I recognized when it was necessary to define words and/or give an example.	1	2	3	4	5
10.	I used visual aids as necessary.	1	2	3	4	5
11.	I used eye contact effectively. That is, I looked at people in all parts of the room.	1	2	3	4	5
12.	I used humor and smiled when appropriate.	1	2	3	4	5

If I could make this speech again, I would _____

_____

What I especially liked about my speech was _____

_____

Additional comments _____

_____

Panel Discussions—Exercise 9A

In a regular informal panel discussion, participants provide information to an audience on a particular topic. When a topic is controversial, the discussion resembles a debate, with participants taking sides or positions. Their discussion is guided by an impartial moderator, who makes sure that everyone has a chance to speak and that the discussion stays on target. This is different from a formal debate, in which each participant speaks for a specified amount of time and there is less spontaneous give-and-take of opinion.

In the informal debate or panel discussion, participants may discuss a controversial subject. Typically, those who have the same position sit together on one side of the moderator and face an audience, as shown below:

(Those in favor of something)	MODERATOR	(Those against something)

A   U   D   I   E   N   C   E

Participants, who express their own opinions or take on special roles, often interrupt each other, which makes it necessary for the moderator to "control traffic." These discussions can become very exciting.

Following a panel discussion, the moderator may invite the audience to ask questions and make comments to the panel members.

The suggested procedure for an informal panel discussion is as follows:

Preparation

1. Each group meets separately to prepare their arguments. They brainstorm their points and make a list, and they also anticipate the points they think the other side will make. The number of panel discussions that go on at the same time will vary according to the size of the class.

2. The moderator plans the introduction. It is helpful for the moderator to think of his or her role as like that of a TV host, who gives background information about the guests and introduces them. The moderator should consult with the teacher about the best way to introduce the subject of the discussion. Once the moderator is ready, if the groups are still preparing, the moderator should visit the groups to get an idea of the points they will raise. This will make it easier for the moderator to prepare some questions in advance. The moderator should always keep in mind that she or he should not express personal opinions in the discussion.

3. If it is possible, arrangements should be made to record the discussion.

Discussion

1. The moderator welcomes the audience, gives the introduction, and then introduces the panel members. (They could wear name tags or have signs on their desks that indicate their names or roles.)

2. The moderator then poses a question to the last panel member that was introduced.

3. The moderator "controls traffic," giving each panel member a chance to complete his or her thought before the next panel member begins speaking. When there is a silence, the moderator breaks in to ask prepared, specific questions to keep the discussion going.

4. The moderator clarifies, summarizes, restates, or paraphrases arguments when necessary. To do this, he or she will have to try to be alert to signs of possible misunderstanding or lack of comprehension on the part of the audience or panel members.

5. The moderator also tries to keep the discussion coherent. That is, if a speaker brings up a point for discussion, and another speaker makes a remark totally unrelated to the subject, the moderator should interrupt and get the discussion back on track.

6. At the end of the allotted time, the moderator summarizes the main points of the discussion. The moderator then asks for questions and/or comments from the audience and continues to "control traffic."

USEFUL PHRASES IN A PANEL DISCUSSION

MODERATOR	PANEL MEMBERS
To introduce a speaker and control traffic, say:	**To "get the floor," say:**
I'd like to introduce . . .	Excuse me for interrupting, but . . .
Let's start with . . .	That's true, but . . .
First __ will speak, and then__	Yes, but . . .
Please don't speak out of turn!	I'd like to make a point here.
I think __ has a question.	I'd like to ask a question.
Now our panel will take questions from the audience.	I have a question for . . .
Sorry to cut you off, but . . .	I'd like to comment on that.
To restate, say:	**To express total agreement, say:**
If I understand, your idea is that . . .	Exactly.
So, you're saying...	That makes sense to me.
In other words, you believe that . . .	That's how I feel about it, too.
Then, ask:	
Is that right?	
Is that what you mean?	
To reflect, say:	**To express partial agreement, say:**
So, your opinion is that . . .	Yes, but...
So, you feel that . . .	Yes, but on the other hand, . . .
You thought it was . . .	That may be true, but . . .

USEFUL PHRASES IN A PANEL DISCUSSION (*Continued*)

MODERATOR	PANEL MEMBERS

To summarize, say:

In summary, then, you think…

These, then, are the ideas that
    you have expressed:

To express total disagreement, say:

I don't agree.

I disagree with…

I don't see it that way.

On the contrary, . . .

To clarify, ask:

Who? What? Where? When?

Why? How? How much/many?

To express your opinion, say:

As I see it, …

From my point of view, . . .

I (firmly/strongly) believe, think, feel . . .

In my opinion, . . .

To get back onto the topic, say:

We've gotten off on a tangent. Let's
    get back on topic.

That's not related to ___. We need
    to talk about ___.

**If you don't understand what
you've heard, say:**

I'm sorry. I didn't catch that.

I'm sorry. I didn't get the part about . . .

Could you please repeat . . .

I'm sorry. I'm not following you.

I'm sorry, but I'm lost.

I didn't understand your question.
    Could you please rephrase it?

To respond to an irrelevant remark:

That doesn't relate to what ___ just said.

To stall (give yourself time), say:

That's a good/interesting/difficult question.
Let me think about it.

To check for comprehension:

Are you following me?

Do you know what I mean?

Does this make sense?

Guest Speakers—Exercise 9A

Before the Visit

1. Your teacher will contact the possible speaker and invite him or her to your class.

2. Once the visit has been arranged, decide as a class on a master list of questions you would like to ask. Send this list to the speaker. (Guest speakers can get nervous too, and knowing ahead of time what the audience is interested in will make your guest more comfortable.)

3. Choose a student to contact the speaker and get information for a one-minute speech of introduction. The student should find out where the speaker is from, what job he or she has, and so on, and then should prepare easy-to-read notes on an index card.

   The student "introducer" should include some of the following phrases in the speech of introduction:

   - I would like to introduce our guest speaker, ____.
   - I am very pleased to introduce ____.
   - ____ is originally from ____.
   - ____ is currently ____.
   - ____ is going to speak to us about ____.
   - Everyone, please welcome ____.

During the Visit

4. The designated student should introduce the guest to the class.

5. Everyone should use active listening skills (nodding, eye contact, etc.) and take notes as they listen to the speaker's presentation. It is possible that the speaker will ask the class comprehension questions to make sure that everyone is following what is being said.

6. During the question-and-answer session that should follow the presentation, students should refer to the list of questions that they prepared ahead of time. They should also feel free to come up with new questions and comments. Questions can be related to the content of the presentation, or they can be used to ask for clarification.

After the Visit

7. The class should do the following:

   - Discuss how well they understood the presentation and what aspects of the speaker's style increased or decreased their comprehension.
   - Write a summary of and reaction to the main points that were covered.

8. One student should send the visitor a thank-you note on behalf of the entire class.

Contact Assignments—Exercise 9B

It would be a good idea, at least at first, if you do this exercise with a partner. If you are prepared and know what to say when you approach someone, you will most likely have a very positive experience.

Here are the guidelines you should follow:

1. Find out where you can find people to talk to. You might approach people at school, at a local store or library, or in your neighborhood. This might be your chance to start conversations with people that you see occasionally but don't know well. You do not have to and should not approach complete strangers on the street.

2. Explain to the people you talk to what you are doing and why, and tell them that your questions will be brief. You might want to start by saying something like this:

    > "Excuse me, I'm from __, and I'm studying English. For homework I'm supposed to find out the meanings of some idiomatic expressions, and I wonder if you would mind answering a few questions."

    You might be surprised to find out that most native speakers of English have never heard of the label "phrasal verbs," although they use these expressions frequently.

    Most people will be happy to answer your questions, especially once they know that you are working on a class assignment. If you have trouble understanding what a person says, don't hesitate to ask for repetition or clarification. Just say, "Could you please repeat that?" or "Could you possibly give me (us) an example?"

Expression Collection—Exercise 10

Directions

1. Find three expressions per week outside of class. These expressions may come from:

   - what you hear on TV, on the radio, in the movies, and in general conversation.
   - what you read in newspapers, magazines, books, advertisements, and on the Internet, billboards, signs, T-shirts, bumper stickers, etc.

2. Keep your collection growing, either in your notebook or on index cards.

3. Follow the format indicated below. If you wish, ask others to explain the expressions that you collect. (Refer to Appendix F for how to approach people to answer your questions about English.)

4. If time permits, you may be asked to teach your classmates some of the expressions that you collect.

Expression: _____

Where I heard it: _____

_____

_____

Who said it:
(indicate whether male or female and approximate age)

_____

_____

Sentence with the expression: _____

_____

_____

What I think the expression means: _____

_____

_____

Student Self-Evaluation Questionnaire

Name (Optional): _____ Date: _____

It is valuable to occasionally stop and reflect on your learning. Below, circle the number that shows how much you agree or disagree with the statement on the left.

	Disagree strongly				Agree strongly
1. My knowledge of idiomatic expressions has increased.	1	2	3	4	5
2. I occasionally try to use some of these expressions when I speak.	1	2	3	4	5
3. When I listen to native speakers of English, I listen for expressions that I have been studying.	1	2	3	4	5
4. When I see or hear expressions that I don't know, I write them down and ask what they mean.	1	2	3	4	5
5. My general knowledge of pronunciation has increased.	1	2	3	4	5
6. I consciously try to monitor (listen to and correct) my pronunciation.	1	2	3	4	5
7. When I listen to native speakers of English, whether in person, on TV, or in the movies, I actively listen for how they use the pronunciation that we've been studying in class.	1	2	3	4	5
8. I'm working hard both in and out of class.	1	2	3	4	5
9. I find studying with others in and out of class to be helpful.	1	2	3	4	5
10. My confidence in my ability to speak English has increased.	1	2	3	4	5

Questions/Comments? _____

_____

Guide to Pronunciation Symbols

Vowels			Consonants		
Symbol	Key word	Pronunciation	Symbol	Key word	Pronunciation
/ɑ/	hot	/hɑt/	/b/	boy	/bɔɪ/
	far	/fɑr/	/d/	day	/deɪ/
/æ/	cat	/kæt/	/ʤ/	just	/ʤʌst/
/aɪ/	fine	/faɪn/	/f/	face	/feɪs/
/aʊ/	house	/haʊs/	/g/	get	/gɛt/
/ɛ/	bed	/bɛd/	/h/	hat	/hæt/
/eɪ/	name	/neɪm/	/k/	car	/kɑr/
/i/	need	/nid/	/l/	light	/laɪt/
/ɪ/	sit	/sɪt/	/m/	my	/maɪ/
/oʊ/	go	/goʊ/	/n/	nine	/naɪn/
/ʊ/	book	/bʊk/	/ŋ/	sing	/sɪŋ/
/u/	boot	/but/	/p/	pen	/pɛn/
/ɔ/	dog	/dɔg/	/r/	right	/raɪt/
	four	/fɔr/	/s/	see	/si/
/ɔɪ/	toy	/tɔɪ/	/t/	tea	/ti/
/ʌ/	cup	/kʌp/	/tʃ/	cheap	/tʃip/
/ɛr/	bird	/bɛrd/	/v/	vote	/voʊt/
/ə/	about	/ə'baʊt/	/w/	west	/wɛst/
	after	/'æftər/	/y/	yes	/yɛs/
			/z/	zoo	/zu/
			/ð/	they	/ðeɪ/
			/θ/	think	/θɪŋk/
			/ʃ/	shoe	/ʃu/
			/ʒ/	vision	/'vɪʒən/

Lesson Answer Key

Lesson Answer Key includes:

- As You Listen
- After You Listen
- Your Turn Listening Challenge answers
- Exercises 1, 2, 3, and 4

Lesson 1

As You Listen

- Bill wants to meet Elizabeth.
- Al encourages his friend to go over and start a conversation.

After You Listen

(A) F, F, F, T, ?

(B) have the guts; give it a shot; skip it; That'll be the day.; pass up

Your Turn: Listening Challenge Script

They are talking about opening a restaurant.

Script:

PART A
A: Are you going to do it?
B: Well, I'm still not sure. I don't know if I should.
A: What are you waiting for? You've saved enough money and your family thinks it's a great idea.
B: But what if it's not successful? Then I'll lose all that money!
A: Come on. You'll be fine. You know what you're doing. You've been planning this for years, you've taken a lot of classes, this is something you've always wanted to do. Give it a shot!

PART B
B: Well, I guess it's the right thing to do. I really don't like working in an office, and I love cooking and being around people. Maybe I should name the restaurant after you!

Exercises

1. Mini-dialogues

   1 A/B: e, a, f, d, b   **2 A/B:** e, a, f, b, d

2. Grammar practice (In some cases, different answers may be possible.)

1. a. He doesn't have the guts <u>to talk (speak)</u> to the teacher.
   b. You're bound <u>to laugh</u> a lot if you see that comedy.

2. a. They wouldn't be caught dead <u>climbing</u> that mountain.
   b. I don't want to pass up <u>going</u> to L.A.
   c. Don't put off <u>celebrating</u> your birthday.

3. a. Give it <u>a</u> shot!   Bite <u>the</u> bullet!
   b. That'll be <u>the</u> day!   Take <u>the</u> initiative!

4. a. Yesterday I finally <u>got</u> something off my chest. I <u>bit</u> the bullet and told my friend the truth.
   b. She <u>took</u> the initiative and started a conversation. They really <u>hit</u> it off and fell in love.
   c. He <u>kept</u> his feelings bottled up for a long time. He always <u>put</u> off telling her the truth.

5. a. They put off their vacation. →   They put <u>it</u> off.
   b. I passed up the cookies. →   I passed <u>them</u> up.

3. Error correction

1. I put off <u>doing</u> my laundry, and now I have nothing to wear.

2. A: Don't you have homework to do?
   B: Uh-huh. I'll do it later.
   A: Don't put <u>it off.</u> Do it now!

3. They met at a party last week and <u>hit</u> it off.

4. If you want a new job, then take <u>the</u> initiative and send your resume everywhere.

5. You <u>are</u> bound to understand more English if you learn a lot of idioms.

6. She doesn't want to pass ✗ up this great opportunity.

7. She doesn't want to pass this opportunity up. CORRECT

8. I wouldn't be caught dead <u>having</u> a pet snake.

9. They didn't have the guts <u>to</u> ski down that mountain.

10. At first, he was afraid to talk to her. But then he gave it <u>a</u> shot.

4. Choosing the idiom

1. What's eating you?
2. don't have the guts to
3. hit it off
4. wouldn't be caught dead
5. pass up
6. is bound to
7. get off your chest
8. bite the bullet
9. put it off
10. Give it a shot.
11. That'll be the day!

As You Listen

They are upset because:

I. some parents aren't keeping their son under control.

2. the restaurant is very noisy.

3. they don't have their food yet.

The couple is more upset. The waitress says it's part of the job.

After You Listen

(A) T, F, T, ?, ?

(B) all of a sudden; put up with; the bottom line is that; is taking forever; have a clue

Your Turn: Listening Challenge Script

Possible answers:

I. The bottom line is that we love each other and we're going to spend our lives together.

The bottom line is that we can't live without each other.

2. The bottom line is that you need to make some changes if you want to keep this job.

The bottom line is that you need to come to work on time and work hard if you want to work here.

The bottom line is that you're going to lose your job if you don't make some changes.

Situation I
Dad, please listen to me. I know we're young, but we've known each other since we were three. We played together, and then we went to school with each other for twelve years. We didn't see each other very often after we graduated from high school, but we really missed each other. Now we don't want to be apart. I know that you and Mom think we should wait, but we want to get married now.

Situation 2
I need to talk to you Andy. I've noticed that you've been coming in to work late every day. First it was a few minutes late, then it was about ten minutes late, and it seems to be getting worse. When you're here, you look tired and sometimes I think you're not concentrating on what you're doing. Honestly, I'm very disappointed because I thought you were perfect for this job when I hired you.

Exercises

1. Mini-dialogues

1 A/B: e, g, a, f, c, b   **2 A/B:** g, a, b, f, c, h, d

2. Grammar practice (In some cases, different answers may be possible.)

1. a. All of <u>a</u> sudden, the alarm went off.

   b. We're planning a surprise party for him, and he doesn't have <u>a</u> clue.

   c. <u>The</u> bottom line is that nothing is forever and we have to appreciate each day.

2. a. I don't want to go through the trouble <u>of</u> doing all this research for nothing.

   b. The police came because the crowd was out <u>of</u> control.

   c. I don't understand why you did that <u>at</u> all.

   d. All <u>of</u> a sudden, she got up and left the room.

   e. I don't have a clue <u>about</u> what she was talking about.

   f. She has no problem putting up <u>with</u> all the mess in her house. She's very relaxed about it.

   g. You always drive. <u>For</u> once, I'd like to drive.

   h. I don't mind dogs. I have nothing <u>against</u> them. But I would never have one.

   i. The babysitter made sure that everything was <u>under</u> control before the parents returned.

   j. I need to do my work <u>in</u> peace. Can you please close the door?

3. a. We stayed in a boring little town. There was nothing at all <u>to do</u> on Saturday night.

   b. It took him forever <u>to learn/to figure out</u> how to use that new computer program.

4. a. I went through the trouble of <u>getting/collecting/writing down</u> everyone's e-mail address, and then I lost the list!

   b. How can you put up with <u>living</u> here? It's so noisy and polluted!

   c. He has nothing against students <u>speaking</u> their native languages with each other. But he doesn't want them to do that in class.

3. Error correction

1. All of <u>a</u> sudden, the lights went out.

2. It took forever to cook this, but it's delicious.   CORRECT

3. She <u>has</u> nothing against using e-mail, but she'd rather write letters. (OR: She doesn't have anything against . . .)

4. <u>The</u> Bottom line is that life is short.

5. Look! Here <u>comes</u> Bill!

6. Look! Here <u>he</u> comes!

7. Look! Here they <u>come</u>!

8. I'm so confused. I don't have a clue <u>about</u> what the teacher said today.

9. He went through the trouble of <u>getting</u> ready for the picnic, but then it rained.

10. We <u>didn't like</u> the concert at all.

4. Choosing the idiom

1. all of a sudden
2. under control
3. at all
4. in peace
5. didn't have a clue that
6. put up with
7. The bottom line is that

Lesson 3

As You Listen

- Jan is bored in her class because there's no discussion, just a lecture.
- Steve is interested in his class because his professor is great. She's interesting and enthusiastic, and she allows discussion in the class.

After You Listen

(A) F, T, ?, T, F

(B) What a drag!; bombed; take you up on; it dawned on me; once in a blue moon

Your Turn: Listening Challenge Script

He doesn't want to go to the party because he can't dance.

PART A

A: I'm sorry, but I really can't go to the party.

B: But it'll be so much fun. You work too much and really need a break.

A: I know, but I'm kind of tired. I think I'd like a quiet weekend.

B: That doesn't sound like you. Come on, tell me the real reason why you won't go.

PART B

A: Well, the truth is, I don't know how to dance. It's really embarrassing.

B: Is that it? Is that really why you won't go? I can't believe it!

A: Are you laughing at me?

B: Not at all! But I still want you to come to the party with me. Listen, why don't I come over on Saturday afternoon and teach you how to dance.

A: No one will see?

B: I promise. No one will even *know*.

A: Hmm. Well . . . OK. I think I'll take you up on that. It's about time that I learn.

Exercises

1. Mini-dialogues

   1 A/B: d, a, b, f, c   **2 A/B:** a, f, e, c, d   **3 A/B:** f, e, a, d, b

2. Grammar practice

   I. a. What <u>a</u> drag! We missed the movie!

      b. We eat out once in <u>a</u> blue moon.

      c. I like studying idioms <u>an</u> awful lot.

   2. a. That book sparked my interest <u>in</u> art history.

      b. We wandered <u>around</u> the city for a while, and then we went to lunch.

      c. I was so scared that I was <u>on</u> the edge <u>of</u> my seat during the whole movie.

      d. It dawned <u>on</u> us that we needed to buy a gift.

      e. What is comes down <u>to</u> is that we need to get more exercise.

      f. I'm not using a recipe. I'm just fooling around <u>with</u> some interesting ingredients.

      g. The kids are fooling around <u>in</u> the backyard.

      h. If you really want to help me, I'd be happy to take you up <u>on</u> your offer.

3. a. We <u>were</u> bored to death at the party, so we left early.

   b. I'm not going to go home yet. I <u>am going to stick</u> it out until the end.

   c. What did he say? My mind <u>was wandering</u>, so I don't know what he's talking about.

   d. You kids <u>have been fooling</u> around since you got home. It's time to sit down and do your homework.

3. Error correction

1. The last election sparked my interest <u>in</u> politics, so I'm going to study political science.

2. What <u>a</u> drag! It's raining, so we can't have the party outside.

3. We've had <u>an</u> awful lot of rain lately.

4. They said they <u>were</u> bored to death at the baseball game yesterday.

5. Be careful. Your wallet is sticking <u>X</u> out of your pocket.

6. Their daughter fools around too much <u>with</u> her friends and doesn't study enough.

7. Yesterday it dawned <u>on</u> me why you really don't want to take that job.

8. We took him up <u>on</u> his offer and went sailing yesterday. It was great.

9. What it comes down to is that they don't pay enough attention to her. CORRECT

10. They're very busy. They can take a vacation only once <u>in a</u> blue moon.

4. Choosing the idiom

1. once in a blue moon	4. an awful lot of	7. it dawned on
2. bored to death	5. buckle down	8. stick it out
3. on the edge of my seat	6. mind was wandering	9. fooled around

Lesson 4

As You Listen

- No, the homeless man hasn't always been poor.
- His wife was unhappy because he worked too much and didn't have time for their family.

After You Listen

(A) F, T, F, ?, T

(B) dead wrong; closed down; day in and day out; this neck of the woods; let up

Your Turn: Listening Challenge Script

Ruth keeps moving up the ladder because she works a lot—she usually works late and takes work home.

JOE: Hey, Ruth! I hear you just got another promotion. Congratulations!

RUTH: Thanks Joe.

JOE: How do you do it?

RUTH: Do what?

JOE: Keep moving up the ladder? You haven't been here that long.

RUTH: Well, I guess I work a lot. Actually, it feels like I work all the time. I usually work late, and on weekends I take work home.

JOE: Sounds like you're a workaholic. Be careful or you might burn out!

RUTH: I know, but I have plans to keep moving up in this company. You know there aren't many women at the top. And I have the time now because I don't have a family yet.

JOE: So, what's going to happen when you have a family?

RUTH: That's an interesting question, my friend. What do YOU think?

Exercises

1. Mini-dialogues

   1 A/B: e, a, c, f, b, h, d   **2 A/B:** h, a, f, d, e, b, c

2. Grammar practice

   I. a. What are you doing in this neck of <u>the</u> woods?

      b. If you want to move up <u>the</u> ladder, work hard!

   2. a. Day <u>in</u> and day out, we study English.

      b. Our friendship is <u>at</u> stake. Let's talk!

      c. So many people live <u>from</u> paycheck <u>to</u> paycheck.

      d. If my grandmother knew, she'd turn over <u>in</u> her grave.

      e. They saved enough money to live <u>on</u> for two years without working!

   3. a. You're doing great work. Keep <u>it</u> up!

      b. They promised to help us move, but they didn't come. They really let <u>us</u> down.

      c. The owners closed down the factory two years ago. → They closed <u>it</u> down.

4. a. After being in the same job for 30 years, he was burned <u>out</u>.

   b. She moved <u>up</u> in the company very fast.

   c. When the rain lets <u>up</u>, let's take a walk.

   d. It's hard to keep <u>up with</u> all this work!

3. Error correction

1. She was <u>burned</u> out so she quit her job.

2. It's hard to live <u>on</u> one salary, so he has two jobs.

3. I eat breakfast <u>day in and day out</u> *every day.*

4. They closed do~~X~~n the store at 5:00 and they'll re-open tomorrow at 10:00.

5. My grade <u>is</u> at stake. I need an 'A' on the next test to keep my average.

6. You can move up the ladder very quickly in this company. CORRECT

7. My friend kept asking me to go to the concert and didn't let ~~X~~ up.

8. My boss said, "You did a great job! Keep ~~X~~ up the good work!"

9. I couldn't keep up <u>with</u> that class, so I changed levels.

10. If she knew, she <u>would turn</u> over in her grave.

4. Choosing the idiom

1. let up

2. keep up with

3. in this neck of the woods

4. at stake

5. That's wishful thinking.

6. <u>D</u>ay in and day out

7. got burned out

8. dead wrong

Lesson 5

As You Listen

- Michael is in shock about winning the lottery.
- He's worried about using the money wisely and not losing it.

After You Listen

(A) F, ?, T, F, T

(B) I haven't the slightest idea.; That's unheard of!; making the most of; you've got it made; What's gotten into

Your Turn: Listening Challenge Script

Mr. Walker is sure that he and his wife were eating tuna sandwiches at 2 o'clock yesterday afternoon.

POLICE OFFICER: OK Mr. Walker. I need to ask you a few questions.

MR. WALKER: Sure. I'll do anything to help.

POLICE OFFICER: Do you know where your wife was at 2 o'clock yesterday afternoon?

MR. WALKER: Yes, she was with me.

POLICE OFFICER: Where exactly were you?

MR. WALKER: Well, we were home, having a late lunch.

POLICE OFFICER: What were you eating?

MR. WALKER: Uh . . . tuna. That's right. We had tuna sandwiches and a salad.

POLICE OFFICER: Are you sure?

MR. WALKER: Yes, beyond the shadow of a doubt. We were eating tuna sandwiches at 2:00 in the afternoon.

POLICE OFFICER: I'm sorry Mr. Walker. I don't think your wife was with you yesterday. She says she was, but you need to get your stories straight. She claims you both had soup yesterday for lunch. I'm afraid I'm going to have to arrest your wife, and you should get a lawyer!

Exercises

1. Mini-dialogues

1 A/B: d, a, e, c, f   **2 A/B:** b, f, a, d, c   **3 A/B:** a, e, b, d, c

2. Grammar practice

1. a. I'm sorry, but I don't have <u>a</u> clue.

   b. I'm sorry, but I don't have <u>the</u> slightest idea.

   c. This grammar is confusing, to say <u>the</u> least.

   d. Back up your work, or it can all go down <u>the</u> drain.

2. a. What's gotten <u>into</u> them?

   b. That can't be true! That's unheard <u>of</u>!

   c. She broke the mirror, and I know what's <u>in</u> store <u>for</u> her!

3. a. When you're in a crowd, be <u>on</u> <u>the</u> lookout <u>for</u> pickpockets.

   b. Try to make <u>the</u> most <u>of</u> your opportunities.

   c. Their plans are still up <u>in</u> <u>the</u> air.

   d. I'm sure, beyond <u>the</u> shadow <u>of</u> <u>a</u> doubt.

4. a. They're very successful. They've <u>got</u> it made.

   b. I haven't <u>got</u> the slightest idea.

   c. What's <u>gotten</u> into them?

   d. I've <u>got</u> to hand it to you. You did a great job!

3. Error correction

1. A: What time is the party?

   B: I don't know. Your guess is <u>as</u> good as mine!

2. A: Can you believe it? He's 40 and he's been married six times.

   B: <u>That's</u> unheard of!

3. A: They're going to have quintuplets? What are they going to do?

   B: I have no idea. They have trouble supporting themselves, <u>let</u> alone five children.

4. A: Does he have a chance of getting the job?

   B: I don't know. He's going to have an interview, so they haven't ruled <u>him out</u>.

5. Can you give me a minute to let this news sink in? CORRECT

6. A: Are you sure? Everyone is going to get a 10 percent raise?

   B: Uh-huh. Beyond <u>the</u> shadow of a doubt.

7. She's been laughing and singing all day. What<u>'s</u> gotten into her?

8. <u>I've</u> got to hand it to you. You did a great job!

9. Idioms are hard to learn, to say <u>the</u> least!

10. I haven't got <u>the</u> slightest idea where I am. I'm totally lost!

4. Choosing the idiom

1. sink in

2. to say the least

3. let alone

4. have it made

5. be on the lookout

6. go down the drain

7. make the most of

8. beyond the shadow of a doubt

9. are up in the air

10. is in store

As You Listen

- Mrs. Calm is handling the situation calmly.
- She tries to get Mr. Claustrophobia to calm down by talking to him and asking him to tell her about himself.

After You Listen

(A) T, T, F, ?, ?

(B) lose your head; out of the blue; sit tight; cooped up in; dwell on

Your Turn: Listening Challenge Script

The last straw	Action taken
1. The roommate took her book.	She moved.
2. Someone thought she was her mother because of her gray hair.	She dyed her hair.
3. He didn't see his son for five days because they were so busy	They're going to talk to each other and make changes so they see each other more. They're going to have dinner together every night.

1. My roommate was horrible! She never cleaned up. She left her clothing and things all over the floor. She even left food around the room! Because she never cared where she put things, she wouldn't be able to find them later. Finally, one day she lost her book, so she took MY book without asking me. That was the last straw. I moved out. I need someone who is respectful of others!

2. I'm only 33, but I'm prematurely gray. I've had gray hair for about five years. I didn't dye my hair because I didn't really want to. Once, some little kids called me "Grandma" and I just laughed it off. Another time a guy I met thought I was older than he was, but it turned out that he was two years older. But I still didn't dye my hair. Not until someone thought I was my sister's mother. That was the last straw. Now I have dark brown hair.

3. My wife and I have four kids. They're 7, 9, 10 and 12. Everyone is busy. After school they have games or piano lessons or something. They're even busy in the evenings. For a long time, we haven't eaten dinner together because of our crazy schedules, and sometimes I feel that I don't know what my kids are doing. Well, last week, I realized that I hadn't seen the 12-year-old for five days! He said he was busy rehearsing for a play. Well, that was the last straw. We're all going to have a talk this weekend and make some changes around here. And we're going to start with having dinner together every night, no matter what.

Exercises

1. Mini-dialogues

   1 A/B: f, d, c, a, b, g   **2 A/B:** c, g, d, f, a, e

2. Grammar practice (In some cases, different answers may be possible.)

   1. a. <u>The</u> last straw was when the car broke down again.
      b. Calm down and keep <u>a</u> level head.
      c. I need to go out. I'm climbing <u>the</u> walls.
   2. a. I need to go out. I've been cooped up <u>in</u> here for too long.
      b. <u>For</u> crying out loud! Please listen to me!
      c. Let's dwell <u>on</u> the good things, OK?
      d. We'll come <u>through</u> this difficult time. Don't worry.
   3. a. She could see him out <u>of the</u> corner <u>of</u> her eye.
      b. I hadn't heard from him in ten years, and then I got a call out <u>of the</u> blue.
      c. Be careful. The boss is really angry. He's <u>at the</u> end <u>of</u> his rope.
   4. a. I knocked myself out all day <u>cleaning (painting)</u> the house.
      b. They were better off <u>living</u> in their old apartment.
      c. Be thankful about where you live now. You'd be worse off <u>living (staying)</u> in that old house.

3. Error correction

   1. The speeding car came out <u>of</u> nowhere.
   2. Out <u>of</u> the corner of my eye, I saw the child sneak a piece of candy.
   3. This is <u>the</u> last straw. I'm not going to go there anymore.
   4. You'd be better off <u>taking</u> three classes instead of four.
   5. I was <u>cooped</u> up the library all weekend because I have three tests this week.
   6. We had a difficult time, but we <u>came</u> through it OK.
   7. It's no use <u>crying</u> over spilt milk! You can't change it.
   8. They had to <u>make</u> do with very little money when they first arrived in this country, but now they're doing fine.
   9. Sit tight <u>and</u> wait until they get here.
   10. He's at the end of his rope. He's going to look for a new place to live. CORRECT

4. Choosing the idiom

   1. cooped up   4. at the end of my rope   6. kept a level head
   2. climb the walls   5. knocking herself out   7. come through
   3. sit tight

As You Listen

- Jason liked the movie.
- They disagree about the use of violence in the movie. Jason thinks it's OK, and Angela thinks there's too much of it and that it's too graphic.

After You Listen

(A) F, T, ?, F, T

(B) It's nothing to write home about.; get through to; a bone of contention; had no bearing on; blowing out of proportion

Your Turn Listening Challenge Script

The woman's argument doesn't hold water because she could have gone outside to use her cell phone to make a call.

A: There you are! I've been waiting for you for three hours. Where have you been?

B: I'm sorry. I was stuck in a meeting and then, when we left, a bunch of people wanted to go out for a drink.

A: So you went?

B: Yeah. I thought it would be quick, but we got into a really serious discussion and I lost track of time. I wanted to call you on my cell phone, but I didn't want to be rude.

A: Oh please. That just doesn't hold water. Everybody uses cell phones and if you were really that worried about what they thought, you could've gone outside for a minute to call me.

Exercises

1. Mini-dialogues

   1 A/B: d, a, f, b, e   **2 A/B:** c, d, e, b, f

2. Grammar practice (In some cases, different answers may be possible.)

   I. a. We can't get through <u>to</u> her. She doesn't listen.

   b. What you said has no bearing <u>on</u> what happened.

   c. Those little kids get away <u>with</u> murder.

   d. <u>From</u> his standpoint, we're wrong.

e. <u>From</u> his point <u>of</u> view, we're wrong.

f. You're blowing this out <u>of</u> proportion.

g. That's a bone <u>of</u> contention <u>between</u> them.

h. The movie was nothing to write home <u>about</u>.

i. We sure got our money's worth out <u>of</u> that TV!

2. a. In this school, students don't get away with <u>cheating (being late)</u>.

b. As far as <u>living (staying)</u> here forever, I'm not sure.

3. a. It wasn't so great. It <u>left</u> a lot to be desired.

b. They <u>lost</u> their bearings in the snow, but they were rescued after a few hours.

c. He got angry and said that she <u>blew</u> everything out of proportion.

d. The music at that party <u>drove</u> me crazy.

e. I was so tired last night that I <u>couldn't keep</u> my eyes open.

3. Error correction

1. The conference wasn't so great. It left a lot to <u>be desired</u>.
   OR: It wasn't anything <u>write home about</u>.

2. When I walked out of the building, I turned right and <u>lost</u> my <u>bearings</u>.

3. You need to take this paragraph out of your essay. It has no bearing on your topic.   CORRECT

4. She thinks she can get away with <u>turning</u> in her homework late all the time, but she's going to have a big surprise.

5. <u>From</u> my point of view, he's getting away with murder.

6. The jury said his argument didn't <u>hold</u> water, so they decided that he was guilty.

7. As far as <u>buying</u> a new car, I think we need to wait and save more money.

8. When I told her that the chicken wasn't cooked enough, she <u>blew</u> it out proportion and said that she was a failure, that she couldn't do anything right.

9. When we couldn't get through <u>to</u> them for two days, we drove over to their apartment to make sure they were OK.

10. A: Why did you leave so early?

    B: Because the music was <u>driving</u> me nuts.

4. Choosing the idiom

1. is driving me up the wall

2. From my standpoint

3. get away with murder

4. left a lot to be desired

5. as far as

6. bone of contention

7. blow this out of proportion

8. get through to

As You Listen

- The daughter was studying in another country.
- Good things that she experienced: she lived in a foreign culture, she went home with her roommate for a holiday; she went to parties and concerts; her fluency and pronunciation improved

After You Listen

(A) T, F, T, F, ?

(B) had ups and downs; stretch out; broach the subject; hopped on; It finally hit home

Your Turn: Listening Challenge Script

1. Hi! I'm Michael. I want to tell you about an incredible opportunity I have. My best friend asked me start a new business with him. He has money from his father to get started, and he wants me to be his partner. We'd split the profits 60-40. When he offered this to me, I couldn't believe it. All I could say was that I'd sleep on it—I didn't want to make my decision then and there. And now that I've slept on it, I'm a bit worried. People say we shouldn't do business with friends, and maybe they're right. I just don't know what to do.

2. Hi! I'm Nancy. I just don't know what to do. Last week, my boss told me that it will be very difficult for me to move up in the company if I stay here, but that I could get a promotion if I move to one of their offices three thousand miles away. Basically, he was asking if I would transfer, and he told me to sleep on it before making my decision. I have such mixed feelings about moving away, but at the same time I want to get more experience. I'm still up in the air and I haven't slept for three days. I need some advice!

Exercises

1. Mini-dialogues

   1 A/B: e, a, f, d, c, g   **2 A/B:** f, a, c, g, e, d

2. Grammar practice

I. a. The kids were tired, but then they got <u>a</u> second wind.

  b. Let's talk some more. We've only just scratched <u>the</u> surface.

  c. I don't want to broach <u>the</u> subject, but I have to.

  d. He was in <u>a</u> rut, but he's OK now because he went back to school.

2. a. Let's talk about this <u>in</u> depth.

  b. Do you need a ride? Hop <u>in</u>!

  c. If you hop <u>on</u> a plane, you'll be there in a few hours.

  d. You got the job? That's music <u>to</u> my ears.

  e. I can't decide now. I have to sleep <u>on</u> it.

3. a. I'm going to bring up the subject later.
   He <u>brought</u> up the subject yesterday.

  b. You slept on it yesterday.
   I <u>am going to sleep</u> on it tonight.

  c. She had her ups and downs when she got home.
   She <u>has had</u> her ups and downs since she got home.

  d. Tell us. We're all ears.
   We <u>were</u> all ears when he told us.

3. Error correction

1. When the teacher saw that he <u>couldn't</u> keep <u>his</u> eyes open, she didn't know if he was tired, or if the class was boring.

2. He was so <u>wiped</u> out that he fell asleep in class.

3. I think I'll stretch ~~myself~~ out for a few minutes.

4. That ten year old kid's a genius. He can do advanced math, and he knows college-level chemistry. To top that off, he can speak nine languages! CORRECT

5. My uncle is 95! He has his <u>ups</u> and <u>downs</u>, but he's OK.

6. Everyone was getting tired before the break, but then we all <u>got a</u> second wind.

7. When I got out of the plane, it <u>hit</u> me that I was really there.

8. Did you make your decision? You said you would <u>sleep</u> on it.

9. She's in <u>a</u> rut. She needs a change in her routine.

10. A: Did you talk about it when you saw her?
   B: No, I didn't <u>bring it up</u> because she was in a hurry.

4. Choosing an idiom

1. wiped out

2. get over jet lag

3. get a second wind

4. hopped on

5. am all ears

6. scratch the surface

7. It hit home

8. had my ups and downs

Review Answer Key

Lessons 1 and 2

1. have nothing against
2. all of a sudden
3. keep someone under control
4. in peace
5. take forever
6. be out of control
7. be bound to
8. the bottom line
9. here she comes
10. skip it
11. skip over
12. bite the bullet
13. put off
14. put up with
15. pass up
16. nothing at all
17. be bottled up
18. hit it off
19. not have a clue
20. go through the trouble of planning

Lessons 3 and 4

1. buckle down/up
2. close down
3. keep up with
4. keep it up
5. an awful lot
6. fool around
7. live on
8. live from hand to mouth
9. once in a blue moon
10. day in and day out
11. at stake
12. what it comes down to is that
13. be burned out
14. it dawned on me that
15. be dead against
16. let someone down
17. move up the ladder
18. on the edge of my seat
19. stick out
20. take you up on your invitation

Lessons 5 and 6

1. out of the blue
2. climb the walls
3. better off
4. cooped up
5. sink in
6. dwell on
7. spilt milk
8. knock yourself out
9. rule out
10. make the most of
11. worse off
12. haven't got the slightest idea
13. sit tight
14. be on the lookout
15. not have a clue
16. down the drain
17. the last straw
18. come through
19. make do
20. up in the air

Lessons 7 and 8

1. it hit home
2. get away with
3. be wiped out
4. drive someone up the wall
5. as far as I know
6. in depth
7. sleep on it
8. get through to someone
9. a bone of contention
10. hop in
11. I'm all ears
12. get my money's worth
13. bring up a subject
14. leave a lot to be desired
15. to top that off
16. stretch out
17. blow something out of proportion
18. nothing to write home about
19. have no bearing on
20. get over jet lag

Crossword Puzzle Solutions

Lessons 1 and 2

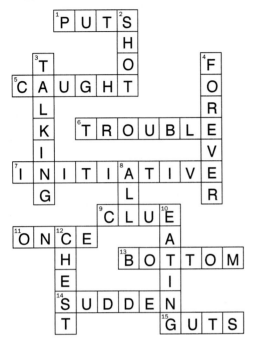

Lessons 3 and 4

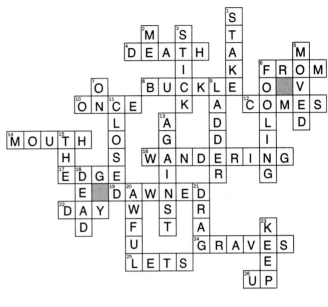

Lessons 5 and 6

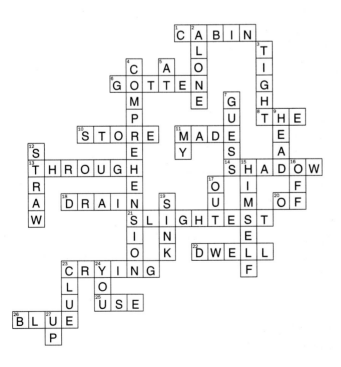

Lessons 7 and 8

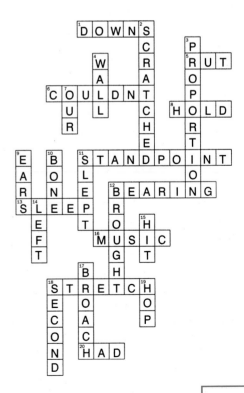

Pronunciation Answer Key

Practice 1

	Usually stressed	Usually unstressed		Usually stressed	Usually unstressed
Nouns	✓		Negative helping verbs	✓	
Pronouns		✓	Adjectives	✓	
Possessive adjectives		✓	Adverbs	✓	
Main verbs	✓		Conjunctions		✓
Verb *be*		✓	Prepositions		✓
Phrasal verbs (1st part)		✓	Articles		✓
Phrasal verbs (2nd part)	✓		*this/that/these/those*	✓	
Affirmative helping verbs		✓	*Wh* question words	✓	

Practice 3B

1. A: We <u>went</u> through the <u>trouble</u> of <u>arranging</u> for them to <u>meet</u>, but <u>neither</u> of them <u>wanted</u> to <u>come</u>.
   B: <u>So</u> <u>what</u> did you <u>do</u>?

2. A: <u>Where</u> are you <u>going</u>?
   B: To the <u>library</u>. I <u>need</u> to <u>study</u> in <u>peace</u>.

3. A: We <u>always</u> <u>go</u> <u>camping</u>. <u>Why</u> don't* we <u>stay</u> at a <u>hotel</u> for <u>once</u>?
   B: <u>Because</u> it's <u>too</u> <u>expensive</u>. <u>You</u>** <u>know</u> <u>that</u>!

*Don't *isn't stressed when "Why don't . . ." is part of a suggestion.*
**Pronouns *are sometimes stressed when the speaker wants to give emphasis.*

4. A: Is he <u>OK</u>?
   B: <u>Yeah</u>, he's <u>fine</u>. It <u>took</u> me <u>forever</u> to <u>reach</u> him <u>because</u> of the <u>storm</u>, but <u>finally</u> I <u>got</u> <u>through</u>.*

*Get through *is a phrasal verb and the preposition* through *is stressed.*

5. A: <u>How</u> do you put <u>up</u> with <u>all</u> <u>that</u> <u>noise</u> <u>upstairs</u>?
   B: It's <u>hard</u>, but I <u>have</u> <u>no</u> <u>choice</u>.

6. A: <u>Why</u> <u>don't</u> you <u>want</u> to <u>come</u> to the <u>concert</u>? You <u>know</u> I <u>have</u> <u>free</u> <u>tickets</u>.
   B: I <u>know</u>, and I <u>don't</u> <u>have</u> <u>anything</u> against <u>classical</u> <u>music</u>. But it <u>always</u> <u>puts</u> me to <u>sleep</u>.

7. A: <u>These</u> <u>kids</u> are <u>out</u> of <u>control</u>. They're <u>driving</u> me <u>nuts</u>!
   B: I'll <u>get</u> their <u>parents</u>.

Lesson 7

Practice 1

Base form of verb	Final sound	Past tense	Final *-ed* sound
1. like	/k/	liked	(/t/) /d/ /ɪd/
2. show	/oʊ/	showed	/t/ (/d/) /ɪd/
3. end	/d/	ended	/t/ /d/ (/ɪd/)
4. look	/k/	looked	(/t/) /d/ /ɪd/
5. listen	/n/	listened	/t/ (/d/) /ɪd/
6. want	/t/	wanted	/t/ /d/ (/ɪd/)
7. hope	/p/	hoped	(/t/) /d/ /ɪd/
8. agree	/i/	agreed	/t/ (/d/) /ɪd/
9. start	/t/	started	/t/ /d/ (/ɪd/)
10. disagree	/i/	disagreed	/t/ (/d/) /ɪd/

Practice 2

/t/
Two people went to a violent movie. One of them <u>liked</u> it a lot, and the
/ɪd/   /d/   /ɪd/
other <u>hated</u> it. The movie <u>showed</u> a lot of blood and killing, and it <u>ended</u> with
/t/
probably a hundred people dead. Of course, the person who <u>disliked</u> the movie
/ɪd/   /ɪd/   /d/
<u>wanted</u> to leave as soon as it <u>started</u>, but she <u>agreed</u> to stay because her friend
/ɪd/
<u>wanted</u> to stay.
/t/   /d/
After the movie, they <u>talked</u> for a while. The woman <u>claimed</u> that
/ɪd/   /d/
violence in the media <u>affected</u> the way children <u>behaved</u>*, and gave them
/ɪd/   /d/
examples of how people <u>committed</u> crimes. Her friend <u>listened</u> and said he
/t/
<u>hoped</u> she was wrong.

Don't link consonant and vowel sounds when a comma comes between them.

Lesson 8

Practice 1

Singular noun	Final sound	Plural noun	Final -s sound		
1. trip	/p/	trips	**/s/**	/z/	/ɪz/
2. afternoon	/n/	afternoons	/s/	**/z/**	/ɪz/
3. walk	/k/	walks	**/s/**	/z/	/ɪz/
4. eye	/aɪ/	eyes	/s/	**/z/**	/ɪz/
5. night	/t/	nights	**/s/**	/z/	/ɪz/
6. country	/i/	countries	/s/	**/z/**	/ɪz/
7. surface	/s/	surfaces	/s/	/z/	**/ɪz/**
8. winter	/ər/	winters	/s/	**/z/**	/ɪz/
9. holiday	/eɪ/	holidays	/s/	**/z/**	/ɪz/
10. roommate	/t/	roommates	**/s/**	/z/	/ɪz/
11. class	/s/	classes	/s/	/z/	**/ɪz/**
12. chance	/s/	chances	/s/	/z/	**/ɪz/**

Practice 2

Base form of verb	Final sound	Third person singular form	Final -s sound		
1. know	/oʊ/	knows	/s/	**/z/**	/ɪz/
2. sleep	/p/	sleeps	**/s/**	/z/	/ɪz/
3. take	/k/	takes	**/s/**	/z/	/ɪz/
4. tell	/l/	tells	/s/	**/z/**	/ɪz/
5. stretch	/tʃ/	stretches	/s/	/z/	**/ɪz/**
6. miss	/s/	misses	/s/	/z/	**/ɪz/**
7. think	/k/	thinks	**/s/**	/z/	/ɪz/
8. help	/p/	helps	**/s/**	/z/	/ɪz/
9. live	/v/	lives	/s/	**/z/**	/ɪz/
10. realize	/z/	realizes	/s/	/z/	**/ɪz/**
11. improve	/v/	improves	/s/	**/z/**	/ɪz/
12. lose	/z/	loses	/s/	/z/	**/ɪz/**

Practice 3

      /s/

Kate's asleep, and her mother, Julia, <u>tries</u> /z/ to wake her up and get her to come to dinner. Kate <u>asks</u> /s/ her mother to let her sleep, but her mother <u>knows</u> /z/ that she <u>needs</u> /z/ to get up. Julia <u>decides</u> /z/ that Kate will get up if she <u>keeps</u> /s/ talking to her. First, she <u>asks</u> /s/ Kate about her <u>plans</u> /z/ and <u>tells</u> /z/ her that she <u>hopes</u> /s/ she'll stay home next year. Then she <u>suggests</u> /s/ that Kate tell her about her <u>friends</u> /z/, but Kate <u>says</u> /z/ that she's too tired to talk.

      When Kate <u>asks</u> /s/ her mother to talk about how she has been, Julia <u>confesses</u> /z/ that she has had her <u>ups</u> /s/ and <u>downs</u> /z/. She <u>explains</u> /z/ that with all her <u>kids</u> /z/ gone, the house has been very quiet. Then, when Julia <u>notices</u> /z/ that Kate is starting to fall asleep again, she <u>pulls</u> /z/ the blanket off and Julia <u>laughs</u> /s/. Finally, she <u>gets</u> /s/ up and <u>says</u> /z/, "You won, Mom. What's for dinner?"

Index: Alphabetical List of Idioms and Expressions

The green number refers to the lesson number(s). The black number refers to the page number.